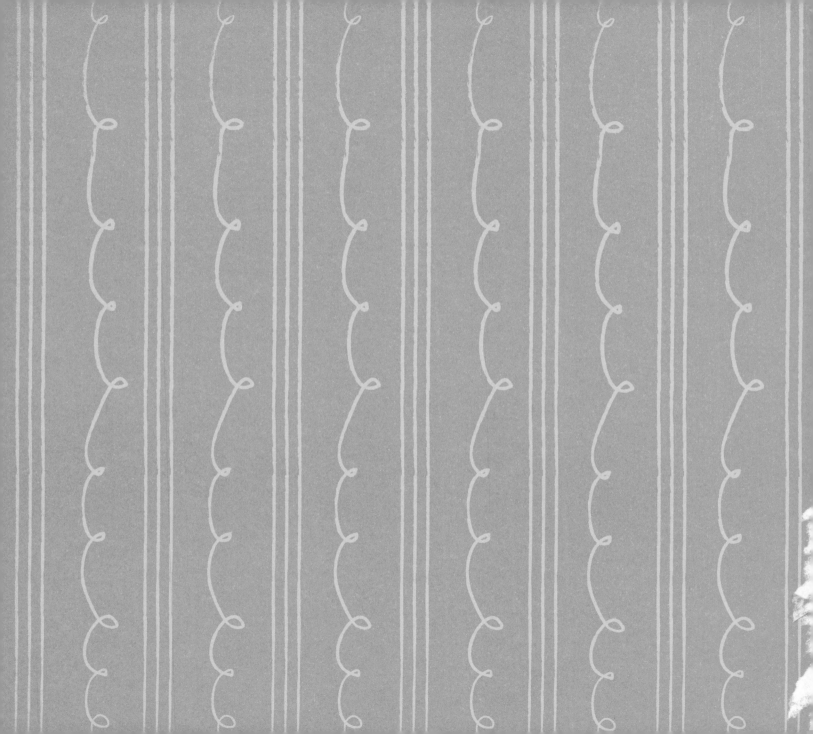

THE *Splenda*® WORLD OF SWEETNESS

# THE Splenda® WORLD OF SWEETNESS

recipes for homemade desserts and delicious drinks

from the maker of SPLENDA® sweeteners

PHOTOGRAPHS BY ALISON MIKSCH

CHRONICLE BOOKS
SAN FRANCISCO

The Library of Congress has cataloged the trade paperback edition:

(ISBN-10: 0-8118-5487-6)

(ISBN-13: 978-0-8118-5487-0)

Cataloging-in-Publication data available.


ISBN-10: 0-8118-5488-4

ISBN-13: 978-0-8118-5488-7


Manufactured in China.

Prop styling by Barbara Fritz

Food styling by Stephana Bottom and Peter Occolowitz (pages 21, 22, 74, 99, 105, 112)

Book design by Level, Calistoga, CA.

2 4 6 8 10 9 7 5 3 1

Chronicle Books LLC

680 Second Street

San Francisco, California 94107

www.chroniclebooks.com

To all the families using SPLENDA® Sweeteners
and to those who specifically requested this book:
Because of your encouragement and endless devotion
to the brand, this cookbook has become a reality.

# contents

# introduction

For many of us, our favorite memories include beloved sweets—enjoying the birthday cake that is so wonderful you press the crumbs from the plate into your fork to savor every last bit, sipping a thirst-quenching glass of ice-cold lemonade during a summer vacation trip, exchanging special holiday treats and cookie recipes that make an appearance only once a year . . . Wherever there are friends and family sharing good times, there is also good food.

However, many great-tasting desserts tend to be high in sugar, which concerns many cooks who want to take pleasure in the baked goods that they serve to their loved ones. By substituting sugar with SPLENDA® Sweeteners, you can feel better about the desserts you share with the people you love.

SPLENDA® No Calorie Sweetener is made from sugar, so it tastes like sugar. Most people begin their familiarity with SPLENDA® Sweeteners through the easily recognizable little yellow packets of SPLENDA® No Calorie Sweetener that they stir into their beverages. But with SPLENDA® No Calorie Sweetener, SPLENDA® Sugar Blend, and SPLENDA® Brown Sugar Blend, today's cooks have a new range of possibilities for creating sweet-tasting desserts with less sugar and fewer calories.

In *The SPLENDA® World of Sweetness*, you'll find cookies for your cookie jar and for holiday gift-giving; luscious cheesecakes and layer cakes to make for special occasions or to bring to potlucks and picnics; simple coffee cakes and quick breads that would be the star of any bake sale or coffee klatch; and juicy, all-American cobblers, crisps, and other old-fashioned fruit desserts, all with a new-fashioned awareness of reducing calories from sugar. You'll find comforting warm desserts and refreshing frozen sweets, satisfying smoothies for healthful snacks, and hot beverages for sipping in front of a fire with a good book.

In the last chapter, you'll find special recipes from some of the best pastry chefs in the country. These chefs have embraced SPLENDA® Sweeteners to create flavorful desserts and other specialties. Their delicious creations may be a bit more challenging and slightly more indulgent than the other recipes in this book, but the end results more than justify the extra time spent in the kitchen.

All of our recipes achieve reductions in calories by substituting SPLENDA® Sweeteners for sugar, and some may have additional improvements in the nutritional profile such as fat reductions. In some recipes the amount of sugar to be replaced is small (such as in icings or toppings), so using SPLENDA® Sweeteners may not result in large calorie reductions, but every small step adds up. Each of our recipes is accompanied by Nutritional Information per serving. Some recipes are higher in calories than others, so if you are watching calories, be sure to check the calorie information to help you keep track. And finally, in addition to the recipes we

share here, you'll also learn how to substitute SPLENDA®
Sweeteners for sugar in your own recipes, with tips on
how to reduce the sugar in all of your dessert-making.

## UNDERSTANDING SPLENDA® BRAND SWEETENER (SUCRALOSE)

SPLENDA® No Calorie Sweetener is a great alternative
to sugar. It gets its sweetness from sucralose (SPLENDA®
Brand Sweetener), which is manufactured by a patented
multistep process that starts with sugar. SPLENDA® Brand
Sweetener is suitable for the whole family.

## ABOUT SPLENDA® NO CALORIE SWEETENER

There are two forms of SPLENDA® No Calorie Sweetener
available.

SPLENDA® Packets are the familiar packets, premea-
sured for sweetening beverages and sprinkling on food.
Each packet provides the sweetness of two teaspoons
of sugar. They can be used to sweeten beverages like
smoothies, shakes, and hot drinks, or to sprinkle on fruit
or cereal.

SPLENDA® Granulated Sweetener is great for cooking
and baking. It measures and pours cup for cup just like
sugar, and works well to replace sugar's sweetness in
cheesecakes, pie fillings, quick breads, muffins, and
cookies. However, its cooking properties are different
from sugar. For example, sugar not only sweetens
desserts, it also provides bulk, contributes to the
spreading of cookie dough, and causes baked goods to
brown. When adapting your own recipes from sugar to
SPLENDA® Granulated Sweetener, some adjustments
should be made. (See the next section for tips on cooking and baking with SPLENDA® Sweeteners.)

## ABOUT SPLENDA® SUGAR BLEND AND SPLENDA® BROWN SUGAR BLEND

A major innovation in the "world of sweetness," and
formulated specifically for home baking, SPLENDA® Sugar
Blend is a unique blend of sugar (sucrose) and SPLENDA®
Brand Sweetener (sucralose). SPLENDA® Sugar Blend has
only half the calories and carbohydrates of sugar on a
per-serving basis. It is excellent in baked goods that rely
on sugar to provide bulk to the batter or dough, as with
layer cakes, quick breads, and cookies.

SPLENDA® Brown Sugar Blend is great when the
flavor and moistness of brown sugar is desired, as in
certain cookies, hot cereals, and sweet side dishes.

Because SPLENDA® Sugar Blend and SPLENDA® Brown
Sugar Blend Products contain sugar, they provide the
taste and baking qualities that you expect from your
favorite recipes, with great moistness, browning, and
rising properties. When used in place of ordinary sugar,
SPLENDA® Sugar Blend and SPLENDA® Brown Sugar
Blend have only half the calories and carbohydrates.

Because SPLENDA® Sugar Blend or SPLENDA® Brown
Sugar Blend are twice as sweet as sugar, when substituting  for sugar or brown sugar, use only half as much as
required by the original recipe. You can also use the
SPLENDA® Sugar Blend and SPLENDA® Brown Sugar
Blend products in unbaked foods and beverages, such
as sprinkling on cereal or sweetening iced tea, but use
only half the amount you are used to. People with dia-
betes should keep in mind that SPLENDA® Sugar Blend
and SPLENDA® Brown Sugar Blend do contain calories
and carbohydrates that should be taken into account
when planning meals.

# Should you wish to adapt your own recipes for SPLENDA®

1. **Volume/Height.** Sugar contributes volume to baked goods. When baking cakes with SPLENDA® No Calorie Sweetener, Granulated, switching from 9-inch round pans to 8-inch round pans with 2-inch-high sides will help achieve a better rise. You may also try adding ½ cup nonfat dry milk powder and ½ teaspoon baking soda for every 1 cup of SPLENDA® Granulated Sweetener.

2. **Creaming.** When creaming butter or margarine with SPLENDA® Granulated Sweetener, the mixture will appear less smooth than with sugar and could look separated. This is normal. The batter will come together when eggs or flour are added.

3. **Texture.** Sugar can play an important role in texture of desserts. For example, some cookies rely on brown sugar for their chewy, crunchy texture. If a recipe includes both brown and white sugar, you have two options. First, you can substitute the brown sugar measurement with SPLENDA® Brown Sugar Blend, using half as much as the brown sugar. (For 1 cup brown sugar, you would use only ½ cup SPLENDA®

Brown Sugar Blend, packing it firmly in the cup just like regular brown sugar; see the chart on page 12.) Or, keep the called-for amount of brown sugar in the recipe, and substitute just the white sugar with an equal amount of SPLENDA® Granulated Sweetener. (Remember; substitute SPLENDA® Granulated Sweetener for sugar cup for cup.)

4. **Thickening.** Sugar lends a thickening quality to jams, jellies, puddings, and custards. When you use SPLENDA® Granulated Sweetener to make these sweets, expect a slightly thinner consistency.

5. **Flavor.** You may wish to enhance the flavor in cookies, pudding, and custards by adding an additional teaspoon of vanilla extract per cup of SPLENDA® Granulated Sweetener.

6. **Moistness.** Sugar helps baked goods stay moist. In muffins and quick breads, the addition of one or two tablespoons of honey or molasses (which are essentially liquid forms of sugar) will provide some moistness as well as flavor.

*Sweeteners, here are some helpful tips:*

**7. Yeast Activation.** SPLENDA® Granulated Sweetener will not activate yeast. Use at least 2 teaspoons of sugar in recipes calling for yeast and replace the remaining sugar with an equal amount of SPLENDA® Granulated Sweetener.

**8. Browning.** Baked goods made with little or no sugar do not brown like those made with sugar. To help achieve a more golden brown color when baking with SPLENDA® Granulated Sweetener, lightly spray the batter or dough with cooking oil spray just before placing in the oven. In some recipes, the addition of a small amount of light corn syrup also enhances browning.

**9. Spread.** As the sugar in cookie dough melts, the cookies spread. Should you substitute all the sugar for SPLENDA® Granulated Sweetener in your cookie recipe, you may need to flatten the cookie dough to the desired width with a fork or the bottom of a flat glass before baking.

**10. Bake Time.** Recipes made with SPLENDA® Granulated Sweetener may bake more quickly than those made with sugar. Check your baked goods for doneness a bit earlier than the original recipe states. For cakes, check 7 to 10 minutes before the end of traditional baking time. For cookies, brownies, and quick breads, check 3 to 5 minutes sooner than usual.

**11. Storage.** Baked goods made with SPLENDA® Sweeteners will stay fresh for 24 hours when stored in an airtight container. For longer storage, wrap well in plastic wrap and an overwrap of aluminum foil (mark the package well with the name of the item and the date) and freeze for up to 3 months.

With SPLENDA® Sweeteners and *The SPLENDA® World of Sweetness*, you can now make great desserts with the sweet taste of sugar your family loves but with less calories.

# substitution chart for SPLENDA® Sweeteners and sugar

| IF YOUR RECIPE CALLS FOR THIS MUCH SUGAR | USE THIS MUCH SPLENDA® NO CALORIE SWEETENER, PACKETS | USE CUP FOR CUP SPLENDA® NO CALORIE SWEETENER, GRANULATED | USE HALF AS MUCH SPLENDA® SUGAR BLEND OR SPLENDA® BROWN SUGAR BLEND |
|---|---|---|---|
| 2 teaspoons | 1 packet | 2 teaspoons | 1 teaspoon |
| ¼ cup | 6 packets | ¼ cup | ⅛ cup (or 2 tablespoons) |
| ⅓ cup | 8 packets | ⅓ cup | 2 tablespoons plus 2 teaspoons (or 8 teaspoons) |
| ½ cup | 12 packets | ½ cup | ¼ cup (or 4 tablespoons) |
| ⅔ cup | 16 packets | ⅔ cup | ⅓ cup (or 5 tablespoons plus 1 teaspoon) |
| ¾ cup | 18 packets | ¾ cup | 6 tablespoons |
| 1 cup | 24 packets | 1 cup | ½ cup |

hot and cold beverages

# banana-peanut chocolate smoothie

This smoothie has a richness almost like a milk shake, making it a very satisfying breakfast drink.
Or enjoy it, one sip at a time, when your energy lags in the middle of the afternoon.

packets

1 small, ripe banana, peeled and sliced
     (see Note)

½ cup nonfat sour cream

3 tablespoons reduced-fat peanut butter

4 packets SPLENDA® No Calorie
     Sweetener

2 teaspoons unsweetened cocoa powder

1 cup crushed ice (see page 16)

### NUTRITIONAL INFORMATION

| | |
|---|---|
| Serving Size: | Sodium: 85 mg |
| ½ cup (4 fl oz) | Total Carbohydrates: 17 g |
| Total Calories: 130 | Dietary Fiber: 2 g |
| Calories from Fat: 45 | Sugars: 7 g |
| Total Fat: 4.5 g | Protein: 5 g |
| Saturated Fat: 1 g | EXCHANGES PER SERVING |
| Cholesterol: 5 mg | ½ starch, 1 fruit, |
| | 1 lean meat |

1. Place the sliced banana on a plate or a piece of aluminum foil and freeze until slightly firm, about 10 minutes.

2. Combine the banana, sour cream, peanut butter, SPLENDA® Packets, and cocoa powder in a blender. Add the crushed ice and process until smooth, stopping occasionally to scrape down the sides of the blender as needed. Serve immediately.

NOTE: Keep a supply of bananas in the freezer—they'll be frozen and ready to use in your next smoothie. Just peel them, cut them into chunks, and put the chunks in zippered plastic bags. You can also freeze whole, unpeeled bananas. The peels will turn black, but the fruit will still be sweet and a fine texture for mixing.

A blender is the best tool for making smoothies. Food processors are sometimes problematic as liquid mixtures tend to flow out of the center tube of a food processor. Immersion blenders, also called handheld blenders—a smaller tool with an extended blade that is immersed in food to blend or purée it—work well with mixtures that don't contain large ice cubes and are treasured for their easy clean-up.

# iced mocha latte

It's hard to beat this caffeinated treat as an afternoon pick-me-up. In fact, you may want to freeze additional coffee cubes in zippered plastic bags to be ready for blending with half-and-half whenever the mood strikes. Made with decaffeinated coffee, it makes a light finale to a summer meal, as well.

**⅔ cup SPLENDA® No Calorie Sweetener, Granulated**

**2 tablespoons unsweetened cocoa powder, preferably Dutch process**

**2 tablespoons instant coffee granules**

**2 cups boiling water**

**2 cups fat-free half-and-half, divided**

**Frozen whipped topping and chocolate curls for garnish (optional)**

**1.** Stir together the SPLENDA® Granulated Sweetener, cocoa powder, and instant coffee in a small bowl. Gradually add the boiling water, whisking until smooth. Stir in 1 cup of the half-and-half. Divide the coffee mixture among ice cube trays. Freeze until completely solid, at least 8 hours or overnight.

**2.** Pour the remaining 1 cup half-and-half into a blender. With the machine running, add the frozen coffee cubes, a few at a time, and blend until smooth. Pour into glasses and serve immediately, topped with a dollop of the whipped topping and the chocolate curls, if desired.

### NUTRITIONAL INFORMATION

Serving Size: 1 cup (8 fl oz) without garnishes
Total Calories: 100
Calories from Fat: 0
Total Fat: 0 g
Saturated Fat: 0 g
Cholesterol: 0 mg
Sodium: 105 mg
Total Carbohydrates: 18 g
Dietary Fiber: <1 g
Sugars: 8 g
Protein: 5 g

**EXCHANGES PER SERVING**
1 starch

# cantaloupe agua fresca

Almost every Mexican market has a stand with large glass urns filled with different varieties of *agua fresca* ("fresh water"), which is fresh fruit blended with water, sugar, and usually a bit of lime juice. The secret to a great *agua fresca* is ripe, flavorful fruit. Here is a basic recipe with cantaloupe, but feel free to use other fruit.

½ ripe cantaloupe, peeled and seeded, flesh cut into cubes

4 cups cold water, divided

⅓ cup SPLENDA® No Calorie Sweetener, Granulated

2 tablespoons fresh lime juice

Crushed ice for serving

1. Process the cantaloupe and 1 cup of the water in a blender just long enough to form a coarse pulp. Transfer to a large pitcher.

2. Add the remaining 3 cups water, the SPLENDA® Granulated Sweetener, and the lime juice and stir to dissolve the SPLENDA®. Serve over the crushed ice.

To make crushed ice, pulse ice cubes in a food processor or blender until the ice is chopped into mostly uniform small pieces.

### NUTRITIONAL INFORMATION

Serving Size:
  1 cup (8 fl. oz)
Total Calories: 30
Calories from Fat: 0
Total Fat: 0 g
Saturated Fat: 0 g
Cholesterol: 0 mg

Sodium: 15 mg
Total Carbohydrates: 7 g
Dietary Fiber: 1 g
Sugars: 5 g
Protein: 1 g

EXCHANGES PER SERVING
½ fruit

# cranberry refresher

You'll find this punch very versatile for autumn and winter entertaining. Chilled, it's a colorful choice for serving at a holiday get-together. Piping hot, sip it in front of the fire after a ski outing. In either case, it can be spiked, if you wish, with a dash of rum, and garnished with a slice of orange or lemon and a cinnamon stick.

8 cups water, divided

2 cups (8 oz) fresh or thawed frozen
   cranberries

8 whole cloves (optional)

1½ cups SPLENDA® No Calorie
   Sweetener, Granulated

1 cup orange juice, preferably fresh

½ cup fresh lemon juice

Crushed ice, if serving cold (see page 16)

1. Bring 2 cups of the water, the cranberries, and the cloves, if using, to a boil in a medium saucepan over high heat. Reduce the heat to medium and simmer until all of the cranberries have popped, about 10 minutes. Strain through a fine-mesh sieve into a large bowl; discard the solids. Add the remaining 6 cups water, the SPLENDA® Granulated Sweetener, orange juice, and lemon juice, and stir to dissolve the SPLENDA®.

2. If serving hot, ladle into cups and serve immediately. To serve cold, cover with plastic wrap and refrigerate until chilled, at least 1 hour; serve over the crushed ice.

## NUTRITIONAL INFORMATION

| | |
|---|---|
| Serving Size: | Sodium: 0 mg |
|   1 cup (8 fl oz) | Total Carbohydrates: 7 g |
| Total Calories: 30 | Dietary Fiber: 1 g |
| Calories from Fat: 0 | Sugars: 2 g |
| Total Fat: 0 g | Protein: 0 g |
| Saturated Fat: 0 g | **EXCHANGES PER SERVING** |
| Cholesterol: 0 mg | ½ fruit |

# vanilla eggnog

Sweet and ultra rich, eggnog may be responsible, for those of us who love it, for a few of those post-holiday pounds. This reduced-fat, reduced-sugar, big-batch version may be slimmed down, but it delivers all the flavor of the traditional version. Here's a family-friendly rendition with vanilla and without alcohol; substitute a teaspoon of rum extract for the vanilla, if you prefer.

**1 cup SPLENDA® No Calorie Sweetener, Granulated**

**1 tablespoon cornstarch**

**1 teaspoon ground nutmeg**

**7 large egg yolks**

**4 cups whole milk**

**2 cups fat-free half-and-half**

**2 tablespoons vanilla extract**

### NUTRITIONAL INFORMATION

Serving Size:
  ½ cup (4 fl oz)
Total Calories: 100
Calories from Fat: 45
Total Fat: 5 g
Saturated Fat: 2 g
Cholesterol: 115 mg

Sodium: 70 mg
Total Carbohydrates: 9 g
Dietary Fiber: 0 g
Sugars: 6 g
Protein: 5 g

**EXCHANGES PER SERVING**
1 reduced-fat milk

1. Stir together the SPLENDA® Granulated Sweetener, cornstarch, and nutmeg in a large, heavy-bottomed saucepan. Whisk the egg yolks in a medium bowl. Gradually whisk the yolks, followed by the milk, into the saucepan.

2. Cook over low heat, stirring constantly and scraping the bottom and sides of the pan with a flat wooden or heatproof silicone spatula, until the custard is thick enough to coat the spatula and an instant-read thermometer inserted in the custard reads 180°F, 5 to 8 minutes. If you want a perfectly smooth eggnog, strain through a fine-mesh sieve into a large bowl. Stir in the half-and-half. Let cool until lukewarm.

3. Cover and refrigerate until the eggnog is chilled, at least 3 hours or up to 3 days. Just before serving, stir in the vanilla. Pour into a chilled punch bowl and serve.

# hot vanilla

Hot chocolate has its many devotees, but what about a warm drink for the legions of serious vanilla fans? This easy, single-serving beverage fits the bill. If you are a true vanilla aficionado, delete the extract and add half a vanilla bean, split lengthwise, to the milk as it warms. Scrape the tiny vanilla seeds from the bean into the milk with the tip of a knife.

**¾ cup fat-free milk**

**2 teaspoons SPLENDA® No Calorie Sweetener, Granulated**

**¼ teaspoon vanilla extract**

### NUTRITIONAL INFORMATION

| | |
|---|---|
| Serving Size: | Sodium: 95 mg |
| ¾ cup (6 fl oz) | Total Carbohydrates: 10 g |
| Total Calories: 70 | Dietary Fiber: 0 g |
| Calories from Fat: 5 | Sugars: 8 g |
| Total Fat: 0 g | Protein: 6 g |
| Saturated Fat: 0 g | **EXCHANGES PER SERVING** |
| Cholesterol: 5 mg | 1 fat-free milk |

1. Heat the milk in a small saucepan over medium heat just until small bubbles appear around the edges of the pan, about 2 minutes. (Alternatively, place the milk in a microwave-safe measuring cup and microwave on High for about 30 seconds.) Remove from the heat and stir in the SPLENDA® Granulated Sweetener and vanilla.

2. Pour into a mug and serve hot.

# lemonade by the glass

Here's the picture—a hammock, a summer afternoon, a good book, and you. To complete this masterpiece, all you need is a glass of cold lemonade. Here's a light recipe for a single, puckery-sweet serving.

**1 large lemon**

**3 packets SPLENDA® No Calorie
   Sweetener**

**Fresh mint leaves (optional)**

**½ cup club soda, chilled, or cold water**

**¾ cup ice cubes**

---

### NUTRITIONAL INFORMATION

| | |
|---|---|
| Serving Size: | Sodium: 30 mg |
| 1 cup (8 fl oz) | Total Carbohydrates: 5 g |
| Total Calories: 20 | Dietary Fiber: 0 g |
| Calories from Fat: 0 | Sugars: 1 g |
| Total Fat: 0 g | Protein: 0 g |
| Saturated Fat: 0 g | EXCHANGES PER SERVING |
| Cholesterol: 0 mg | Free |

**1.** Slice two rounds from the lemon and place in a glass. Squeeze 2 teaspoons lemon juice from the remaining lemon and add to the glass. Add the SPLENDA® Packets and the mint leaves, if using. Using a long spoon, mash the lemon slices and mint together to extract the lemon juice and lightly crush, or "bruise," the mint to release its flavor and aroma.

**2.** Add the club soda and stir. Add the ice and serve.

To keep chilled, fruit-juice-based beverages or punches ice-cold but not diluted, pour some of the mixed punch or the base fruit juices called for in a recipe into ice cube trays and freeze. Serve the beverage poured over the fruit-juice ice cubes. For large batches served in a punch bowl, freeze a portion of the punch or juices in a ring mold; unmold the ring and place in the bowl with the punch when ready to serve.

# lemonade by the pitcher

A large, frosty pitcher of this classic beverage will bring back childhood memories of lemonade stands and sunny summer afternoons. And there are countless ways to expand upon the lemonade theme; a collection of flavorful variations follows the classic recipe. (The nutritional data for the variations does not change significantly.)

**5 cups water**

**1 cup fresh lemon juice (from about 6 lemons)**

**1 cup SPLENDA® No Calorie Sweetener, Granulated**

**Ice cubes for serving**

**Fresh mint sprigs and lemon slices for garnish (optional)**

**1.** Stir the water, lemon juice, and SPLENDA® Granulated Sweetener in a large pitcher until the SPLENDA® dissolves.

**2.** Serve over ice, garnished with the mint and lemon, if desired.

### Variations

**LIMEADE:** Substitute 1 cup fresh lime juice for the lemon juice.

**GINGER-MINT LEMONADE:** Prepare the lemonade as directed but using 4 cups water; set aside. Bring an additional 1 cup water, ⅓ cup loosely packed fresh mint leaves, and 3 tablespoons freshly grated ginger (use the large holes on a box grater) to a boil in a small saucepan over medium heat. Remove from the heat, cover, and let stand for 5 minutes. Strain through a fine-mesh sieve into the lemonade, discarding the solids. Stir well.

**TROPICAL LEMONADE:** Prepare the lemonade as directed but using 3 cups water. Stir in 1 cup unsweetened pineapple juice and 1 cup mango juice.

**BERRY LEMONADE:** Prepare the lemonade as directed but using 3½ cups water. Process 1 cup of the lemonade and 1½ cups fresh or frozen blackberries, raspberries, or strawberries in a blender or food processor. Strain through a fine-mesh sieve into the lemonade, discarding the solids. Stir well.

**WATERMELON LEMONADE:** Prepare the lemonade as directed but using 3 cups water. Purée 3 cups seedless watermelon in a food processor or blender. Stir into the lemonade.

#### NUTRITIONAL INFORMATION

Serving Size:
  ¾ cup (6 fl oz), not
  including variations
Total Calories: 20
Calories from Fat: 0
Total Fat: 0 g
Saturated Fat: 0 g
Cholesterol: 0 mg

Sodium: 0 mg
Total Carbohydrates: 6 g
Dietary Fiber: 0 g
Sugars: 1 g
Protein: 0 g

EXCHANGES PER SERVING
½ fruit

# pomegranate punch

Antioxidant-rich pomegranate juice is now more widely available in bottles and it makes a delicious ingredient in punch. The age-old problem of keeping a chilled punch cold is solved here by adding frozen cubes of orange juice to the pitcher; the juice adds extra flavor, as well. For a big party, double or triple the amount of punch, freeze the orange juice in a large ring mold, and place the frozen ring in the punch bowl.

**2 cups orange juice, preferably fresh**

**3 cups pomegranate juice, chilled**

**½ cup SPLENDA® No Calorie Sweetener, Granulated**

**2 tablespoons fresh lime juice**

**2 cups sparkling mineral water or club soda, chilled**

1. Pour the orange juice into ice cube trays. Freeze until completely solid, at least 4 hours or overnight.

2. Combine the pomegranate juice, SPLENDA® Granulated Sweetener, and lime juice in a large pitcher and stir until the SPLENDA® dissolves. Add the orange juice cubes and stir until the cubes begin to melt. Stir in the sparkling water and serve chilled.

### NUTRITIONAL INFORMATION

| | |
|---|---|
| Serving Size: ¾ cup (6 fl oz) | Sodium: 10 mg |
| | Total Carbohydrates: 30 g |
| Total Calories: 120 | Dietary Fiber: 0 g |
| Calories from Fat: 0 | Sugars: 25 g |
| Total Fat: 0 g | Protein: 1 g |
| Saturated Fat: 0 g | EXCHANGES PER SERVING |
| Cholesterol: 0 mg | 2 fruits |

# mexican spiced coffee

Dark-roast coffee, spices, and a dash of orange juice combine to give this cup of joe an unmistakable Latin flavor. It is an elegant way to finish a dinner with friends, especially one that featured Mexican food. Be sure to offer milk or half-and-half and additional SPLENDA® No Calorie Sweetener so guests can add them to their beverages according to taste.

⅓ cup ground espresso or other dark-roast coffee

¾ teaspoon ground cinnamon

¼ teaspoon ground nutmeg

3 cups water

2 tablespoons SPLENDA® No Calorie Sweetener, Granulated

1 tablespoon orange juice, preferably fresh

1. Combine the coffee, cinnamon, and nutmeg in a coffee filter in an electric coffee maker.

2. Pour the water into the water receptacle. Add the SPLENDA® Granulated Sweetener and orange juice to empty coffee pot; brew. Serve black or with milk and additional SPLENDA®, if desired.

Hot beverages will hold their heat best if served in warmed cups. Fill the cups with very hot tap water and let stand while making the beverage. Discard the water and quickly dry the cups before filling and serving.

### NUTRITIONAL INFORMATION

Serving Size:
  1 cup (8 fl oz)
Total Calories: 30
Calories from Fat: 5
Total Fat: 0.5 g
Saturated Fat: 0 g
Cholesterol: 0 mg

Sodium: 35 mg
Total Carbohydrates: 6 g
Dietary Fiber: 0 g
Sugars: 4 g
Protein: 0 g

**EXCHANGES PER SERVING**
½ starch

# mulled cider

The next time you have a big holiday party, consider a pot of this intriguingly spiced mulled cider, which, as an added benefit, will fill the house with mouthwatering aromas. (Did you know that mulled means "dusted" in seventeenth-century English, as in "dusted with spices"?) To keep the cider warm during the celebration, serve it from a large slow cooker, or place the pot on a hot plate.

**2 quarts unsweetened apple cider**

**½ cup SPLENDA® No Calorie Sweetener, Granulated**

**½ cup dried cranberries**

**⅓ cup fresh lemon juice**

**16 whole cloves**

**6 whole allspice berries**

**Five 3-inch cinnamon sticks, plus more for garnish**

**2 oranges, thinly sliced, plus more for garnish**

**2 lemons, thinly sliced, plus more for garnish**

1. Combine the cider, SPLENDA® Granulated Sweetener, cranberries, lemon juice, cloves, allspice, and 5 cinnamon sticks in a Dutch oven or stockpot over medium heat and bring to a boil, stirring until the SPLENDA® dissolves. Reduce the heat to low and simmer for 20 minutes.

2. Add the oranges and lemons and return to a boil over high heat. Return the heat to low and simmer for 10 minutes longer.

3. Strain the mulled cider into a large saucepan (or a slow cooker, if serving from one) and discard the solids. Serve hot, garnishing each serving with additional orange and lemon slices and cinnamon sticks, as desired.

### NUTRITIONAL INFORMATION

Serving Size: ½ cup (4 fl oz)
Total Calories: 80
Calories from Fat: 0
Total Fat: 0 g
Saturated Fat: 0 g
Cholesterol: 0 mg
Sodium: 19 mg
Total Carbohydrates: 16 g
Dietary Fiber: 0 g
Sugars: 16 g
Protein: 0 g

**EXCHANGES PER SERVING**
1 fruit

# ruby red chiller

Red grapefruit (strikingly darker colored than pink grapefruit) are quite a bit sweeter than yellow grapefruit, and their brilliant color gives this drink plenty of eye-appeal. They are at their best, both in flavor and affordability, from October to May. This refreshing drink would be a colorful addition to a leisurely brunch.

**7 large red grapefruit**

**1 cup tap water**

**1 cup SPLENDA® No Calorie Sweetener, Granulated**

**⅓ cup fresh lemon juice**

**2 cups noncarbonated mineral water or club soda, chilled**

**Fresh mint sprigs and strips of grapefruit zest for garnish (optional)**

NUTRITIONAL INFORMATION

| | |
|---|---|
| Serving Size: | Sodium: 0 mg |
| 1 cup (8 fl oz) | Total Carbohydrates: 15 g |
| Total Calories: 60 | Dietary Fiber: 0 g |
| Calories from Fat: 0 | Sugars: 9 g |
| Total Fat: 0 g | Protein: 1 g |
| Saturated Fat: 0 g | EXCHANGES PER SERVING |
| Cholesterol: 0 mg | 1 fruit |

1. Squeeze the juice from 5 of the grapefruits into a 1-quart measuring cup; you should have about 3 cups. Peel the remaining 2 grapefruit. Using a serrated knife, working over a bowl to catch the juices, cut between the membranes to release the grapefruit sections; transfer each section as it drops free to a cutting board. Coarsely chop the sections and set aside. Add the juice from sectioning the grapefruit to the 3 cups juice.

2. In a large pitcher, combine the grapefruit juice, tap water, SPLENDA® Granulated Sweetener, and lemon juice and stir until the SPLENDA® dissolves. Add the chopped grapefruit. Cover and refrigerate until chilled, at least 4 hours or overnight.

3. When ready to serve, add the mineral water. Pour into glasses, garnish with the mint sprigs and grapefruit zest (if using), and serve chilled.

# southern iced tea

What makes iced tea Southern isn't the type of tea used (that would be good old orange pekoe), but the fact that it is good and sweet. This recipe for the ultimate thirst-quenching beverage makes that assumption, but you can cut back or adjust the SPLENDA® No Calorie Sweetener to taste. And check out the variations on the facing page for a change of pace (keeping in mind that fruit juices will alter the nutritional information a bit).

**5 cups water, divided**

**2 family-sized tea bags (see Note)**

**1 cup SPLENDA® No Calorie Sweetener, Granulated**

**Ice cubes for serving**

**Fresh mint sprigs and lemon slices for garnish (optional)**

### NUTRITIONAL INFORMATION

Serving Size: about ¾ cup (about 6 fl oz), not including variations
Total Calories: 15
Calories from Fat: 0
Total Fat: 0 g
Saturated Fat: 0 g
Cholesterol: 0 mg

Sodium: 0 mg
Total Carbohydrates: 4 g
Dietary Fiber: 0 g
Sugars: 0 g
Protein: 0 g
**EXCHANGES PER SERVING**
Free

1. Bring 3 cups of the water to a boil in a medium saucepan. Add the tea bags and remove from the heat. Cover and let stand for 5 minutes. Remove the tea bags with a slotted spoon, gently squeezing them with another spoon. Discard the tea bags.

2. Add the remaining 2 cups water and the SPLENDA® Granulated Sweetener and stir until the SPLENDA® dissolves. Pour into a large pitcher. Serve over ice, garnishing each serving with the mint sprigs and lemon slices, if desired.

**NOTE:** You can substitute 6 regular-sized tea bags or 2 tablespoons loose tea for the family-sized tea bags. If using loose tea, strain the brewed tea through a fine-mesh sieve into the pitcher.

*Variations*

**CITRUS-MINT TEA:** Add ½ cup loosely packed mint leaves to the boiling water with the tea bags. After steeping as directed, strain through a fine-mesh sieve into the pitcher. Add 1 cup orange juice, preferably fresh, and ⅓ cup fresh lemon juice along with the remaining 2 cups water and the SPLENDA® Granulated Sweetener. Serve over ice, with the mint and lemon, if desired.

**ALMOND TEA:** Prepare and steep the tea as directed. Stir in ⅔ cup fresh lemon juice, 2 teaspoons almond extract, and 1 teaspoon vanilla extract along with the remaining 2 cups water and the SPLENDA®. Serve over ice, with lemon slices, if desired.

**GINGER TEA:** Add ½ cup minced fresh ginger with the tea bags to the boiling water. After steeping as directed, strain through a fine-mesh sieve into the pitcher. Add ½ cup fresh lemon juice along with the remaining 2 cups water and the SPLENDA®. Serve over ice, with lemon slices, if desired.

**PINEAPPLE TEA:** Prepare and steep the tea as directed. Substitute 2 cups unsweetened pineapple juice plus ⅓ cup fresh lemon juice for the 2 cups water.

**CHAI ICE TEA:** Combine 3 cups water, 2 tablespoons minced fresh ginger, two 3-inch cinnamon sticks, 2 teaspoons whole black peppercorns, ½ teaspoon whole cloves, and 6 crushed cardamom pods in a medium saucepan and bring to a boil over high heat. Reduce the heat to medium-low and simmer for 10 minutes. Add 2 family-sized tea bags (see Note), remove from the heat, cover, and let stand for 5 minutes. Strain through a fine-mesh sieve into the pitcher. Add 1 cup SPLENDA®, 1 cup fat-free half-and-half, and 1 cup water and stir until the SPLENDA® is dissolved. Serve over ice.

# sparkling fruit punch

Punch remains the beverage of choice to serve to a crowd at such festive gatherings as weddings and graduations. The original recipes truly "packed a punch" with their alcohol content, but it is wiser to serve a low-octane version and serve liquor on the side so guests can take it or leave it. (This punch would be good with vodka or rum.) Here, a combination of fruit juices comes together to create a punch with classic flavors.

**2 cups cranberry juice cocktail, chilled**

**1½ cups pineapple-orange juice, chilled**

**1½ cups cold water**

**½ cup SPLENDA® No Calorie Sweetener, Granulated**

**1½ cups sparking mineral water, chilled**

**Crushed ice for serving (see page 16)**

1. Combine the cranberry and pineapple-orange juices, cold water, and SPLENDA® Granulated Sweetener in a large pitcher and stir until the SPLENDA® dissolves. Cover and refrigerate until well chilled, about 1 hour.

2. Just before serving, stir in the mineral water. Serve over the crushed ice.

To use any leftover punch or smoothie, pour it into freezer pop molds, add wooden pop sticks, and freeze until solid. Alternatively, freeze leftover smoothie in an air-tight container. When you're ready to serve it, unmold the frozen smoothie and chop it into chunks with a large knife, then process the chunks in a blender with a bit more of any liquid called for in the original recipe (milk, tea, fruit juice). These techniques work best with smoothies made from fresh, not previously frozen, fruit.

### NUTRITIONAL INFORMATION

| | |
|---|---|
| Serving Size: about ½ cup (about 4 fl oz) | Sodium: 0 mg |
| | Total Carbohydrates: 15 g |
| Total Calories: 60 | Dietary Fiber: 0 g |
| Calories from Fat: 0 | Sugars: 13 g |
| Total Fat: 0 g | Protein: 1 g |
| Saturated Fat: 0 g | EXCHANGES PER SERVING |
| Cholesterol: 0 mg | 1 fruit |

special occasion cakes

# pineapple upside-down cake

An all-American classic, pineapple upside-down cake deserves its reputation as one of the best old-fashioned desserts that a baker can produce. And now, with SPLENDA® Sweeteners, it can be made with half the amount of sugar. Maraschino cherries give the cake a "fresh from Grandma's kitchen" look, but omit them if you prefer.

10 tablespoons (1¼ sticks) unsalted butter, at room temperature, divided

½ cup firmly packed SPLENDA® Brown Sugar Blend

One 15½-ounce can pineapple slices in juice, well drained

8 maraschino cherries, drained

¼ cup chopped pecans

2¼ cups sifted cake flour (sifted first, then measured)

⅔ cup SPLENDA® Sugar Blend

1½ teaspoons baking powder

¼ teaspoon baking soda

¼ teaspoon salt

¾ cup low-fat buttermilk

1 teaspoon vanilla extract

¾ cup egg substitute

### NUTRITIONAL INFORMATION

Serving Size: 1 slice
Total Calories: 300
Calories from Fat: 100
Total Fat: 11 g
Saturated Fat: 6 g
Cholesterol: 25 mg

Sodium: 170 mg
Total Carbohydrates: 47 g
Dietary Fiber: 1 g
Sugars: 26 g
Protein: 5 g

**EXCHANGES PER SERVING**
2 starches, 1 fruit, 2 fats

1. Position a rack in the center of the oven and preheat to 350°F.

2. Melt 2 tablespoons of the butter in a 10-inch cast-iron skillet. (Alternatively, use a 10-inch round, heavy-duty metal cake pan with 2-inch sides.) Remove from the heat. Sprinkle the SPLENDA® Brown Sugar Blend evenly in the skillet. Arrange the pineapples and cherries in the skillet, then sprinkle with the pecans.

3. Sift together the flour, SPLENDA® Sugar Blend, baking powder, baking soda, and salt into a large bowl. Add the remaining 8 tablespoons butter. Using a pastry blender, two knives, or an electric mixer on low speed, cut the butter into the flour mixture until the mixture is uniformly crumbly. In a small bowl, stir together the buttermilk and vanilla. Using an electric mixer on low speed, add the buttermilk mixture to the bowl with the flour mixture in three additions, mixing each addition just until blended and stopping occasionally to scrape down the sides of the bowl as needed. During the third addition, add the egg substitute and beat until the batter is smooth, about 30 seconds. Spread the batter evenly in the prepared pan.

4. Bake until a wooden toothpick inserted in the center of the cake comes out clean, 35 to 40 minutes. Let cool on a wire rack for 5 minutes. Run a dull knife around the inside of the pan, then invert the cake onto a round serving platter and remove the pan. Serve warm or at room temperature.

# applesauce gingerbread

This wonderfully spicy and extremely easy cake is also quite moist, thanks to the applesauce that replaces much of the fat in the traditional recipe. It stands on its own, but can also be dressed up with sautéed apples or a dollop of whipped topping. As a simple garnish, try the "Powdered Sugar," if you wish.

**Nonstick cooking spray and flour for the pan**

**2 cups unsweetened applesauce**

**¾ cup unsulfured molasses**

**3 large eggs**

**⅓ cup vegetable oil**

**3 cups all-purpose flour**

**2 teaspoons baking powder**

**1 teaspoon baking soda**

**½ teaspoon salt**

**2 teaspoons ground ginger**

**1½ teaspoons ground cinnamon**

**½ teaspoon ground cloves**

**1⅓ cups SPLENDA® No Calorie Sweetener, Granulated**

**"Powdered Sugar" (recipe follows), optional**

1. Position a rack in the center of the oven and preheat to 350°F. Lightly spray the inside of a 12-cup nonstick fluted tube pan with the cooking spray. Dust the inside of the pan with flour and tap out the excess flour.

2. Whisk the applesauce, molasses, eggs, and oil in a large bowl to combine. Sift together the flour, baking powder, baking soda, salt, ginger, cinnamon, and cloves into a medium bowl. Stir in the SPLENDA® Granulated Sweetener. Add the dry ingredients to the applesauce mixture and stir well. Spread the batter evenly in the prepared pan.

3. Bake until a wooden toothpick inserted in the center of the cake comes out clean, 50 to 60 minutes. Let cool on a wire rack for 20 minutes. If serving warm, invert the cake onto a serving plate and remove the pan. Cut into wedges and serve, dusted with the "Powdered Sugar," if desired. To serve at room temperature, invert onto the rack and let cool completely, then garnish if desired and serve.

**"POWDERED SUGAR":** Combine ½ cup SPLENDA® Granulated Sweetener and 1 tablespoon cornstarch in a blender. Cover tightly and blend until the SPLENDA® is finely ground. Sprinkle over the cake.

### NUTRITIONAL INFORMATION

Serving Size: 1 slice without garnish
Total Calories: 180
Calories from Fat: 45
Total Fat: 5 g
Saturated Fat: 0.5 g
Cholesterol: 35 mg
Sodium: 250 mg
Total Carbohydrates: 31 g
Dietary Fiber: 1 g
Sugars: 11 g
Protein: 3 g

EXCHANGES PER SERVING
2 starches, 1 fat

# pumpkin cake roll
## with cream cheese filling

This easy-to-make, impressive-looking dessert could rival pumpkin pie for the place of honor at your holiday dinner. One of its many attributes is that it can be made ahead and frozen, wrapped well in plastic wrap and then aluminum foil, for up to 1 month. Thaw the roll overnight in the refrigerator before serving.

### Cake

**Nonstick cooking spray and flour for the pan**

**3 large eggs, at room temperature**

**½ cup SPLENDA® No Calorie Sweetener, Granulated, divided**

**¼ cup light corn syrup**

**¾ cup canned solid-pack pumpkin**

**1 teaspoon fresh lemon juice**

**¾ cup all-purpose flour**

**1 teaspoon baking powder**

**½ teaspoon salt**

**2 teaspoons ground cinnamon**

**1 teaspoon ground ginger**

**½ teaspoon ground nutmeg**

**2 tablespoons confectioners' sugar for rolling the cake, plus more for garnish, if desired**

1. Position a rack in the center of the oven and preheat to 350°F. Lightly spray the inside of a 15-by-10-by-1-inch jelly-roll pan with the cooking spray. Line the bottom of the pan with a piece of waxed paper. Grease the waxed paper, dust with flour, and tap out the excess flour.

2. To make the cake, beat the eggs in a large bowl with an electric mixer on high speed until tripled in volume and pale yellow, about 5 minutes. Gradually beat in ¼ cup of the SPLENDA® Granulated Sweetener and the corn syrup and beat for 2 minutes more. Reduce the speed to low and gradually add the pumpkin, then the lemon juice, beating until well combined.

3. Sift together the flour, baking powder, salt, cinnamon, ginger, and nutmeg into a medium bowl. Stir in the remaining ¼ cup SPLENDA®. Gradually fold the flour mixture into the pumpkin mixture. Using a metal spatula, spread the batter evenly in the prepared pan.

4. Bake until the cake springs back when pressed in the center with a finger, about 12 minutes. Let cool for 2 minutes. Sift the 2 tablespoons confectioners' sugar evenly over a clean kitchen towel. Run a dull knife around the inside of the pan to release the cake. Invert and unmold the cake and waxed paper onto the towel. Carefully peel off the waxed paper and then lay it back over the top of the cake. Starting at a short end, using the towel as an aid, roll up the cake with the towel into a thick cylinder. Transfer the towel-wrapped cake to a wire rack, seam side down, and let cool completely.

## Cream Cheese Filling

**One 8-ounce package reduced-fat cream cheese, well softened**

**4 tablespoons unsalted butter, softened**

**½ teaspoon vanilla extract**

**½ cup SPLENDA® No Calorie Sweetener, Granulated**

**½ cup "Powdered Sugar" (see page 36), plus more for garnish (optional)**

### NUTRITIONAL INFORMATION

| | |
|---|---|
| Serving Size: 1 slice | Sodium: 320 mg |
| Total Calories: 220 | Total Carbohydrates: 26 g |
| Calories from Fat: 100 | Dietary Fiber: 1 g |
| Total Fat: 11 g | Sugars: 15 g |
| Saturated Fat: 7 g | Protein: 6 g |
| Cholesterol: 90 mg | EXCHANGES PER SERVING |
| | 1½ starches, 2 fats |

5. To make the filling, beat the cream cheese, butter, and vanilla in a medium bowl with an electric mixer on high speed until creamy, about 1 minute. Gradually add the SPLENDA® Granulated Sweetener and "Powdered Sugar," beating until blended.

6. To assemble the cake, unroll it and discard the waxed paper. Spread the cream cheese filling evenly over the cake, then reroll the cake. Transfer the cake, seam side down, to a serving platter. Sift additional "Powdered Sugar" over the top, if desired.

7. To serve, using a large serrated knife, slice crosswise on a slight diagonal.

It is best to sift the dry ingredients for a batter together rather than just whisk them to combine. Sifting doesn't just mix and aerate the dry ingredients; it also breaks up the tiny clumps of flour and leavenings that could remain undissolved in the batter, and helps distribute the leavening evenly. If you take the short cut and whisk the dry ingredients, whisk them well, or you run will the risk of having clumps of baking soda, baking powder, or flour in your baked goods. You do not need a special sifter—simply pass the dry ingredients through a coarse-mesh sieve.

# angel food cake

Every baker should know how to make angel food cake, as it is one of the most versatile of all baked goods. Although it is fat free, it is delicious served without any embellishments; or it can be frosted with fat-free whipped topping and garnished with fresh berries to become shortcake, without adding any fat. Be sure to use an ungreased tube pan without an interior coating, as the batter needs a tactile surface in order to climb up the sides of the pan during baking.

**1 cup sifted cake flour (sifted first, then measured)**

**¼ cup cornstarch**

**1 cup SPLENDA® Sugar Blend, divided**

**1½ cups egg whites (from 10 to 12 large eggs)**

**1½ teaspoons cream of tartar**

**1 teaspoon vanilla extract**

**½ cup light corn syrup**

### NUTRITIONAL INFORMATION

Serving Size: 1 slice
Total Calories: 170
Calories from Fat: 0
Total Fat: 0 g
Saturated Fat: 0 g
Cholesterol: 0 mg

Sodium: 70 mg
Total Carbohydrates: 39 g
Dietary Fiber: 0 g
Sugars: 27 g
Protein: 4 g

EXCHANGES PER SERVING
2½ starches

1. Position a rack in the lower third of the oven and preheat to 350°F. Have ready an ungreased 10-inch tube pan (not nonstick) with a removable bottom.

2. Sift together the sifted cake flour and cornstarch onto a sheet of waxed paper, then sift a second time into a bowl. Stir in ¾ cup of the SPLENDA® Sugar Blend.

3. Beat the egg whites in a large bowl with an electric mixer on high speed until foamy. Add the cream of tartar and vanilla and continue beating until the whites form soft peaks. Gradually beat in the corn syrup and the remaining ¼ cup SPLENDA® until the whites form stiff, shiny peaks.

4. Sprinkle one-fourth of the flour mixture over the whites and gently fold it in with a large rubber spatula. Repeat three more times with the remaining flour mixture. Scrape the batter into the pan and spread evenly. Insert a knife into the batter and run it through the batter in a zigzag pattern to break any air bubbles.

> CONTINUED

**5.** Bake until the cake springs back when lightly touched, 40 to 45 minutes. Invert the cake pan on a work surface. (To maintain their texture, angel food cakes are cooled upside down in the pan. Most tube pans with removable bottoms have small "feet" or a long center tube that holds the inverted pan above the work surface during cooling so moisture does not collect. If yours doesn't have one, balance the edges of the inverted pan on three coffee mugs, turned upside down and spaced equally apart.) Let the cake cool completely.

**6.** Set the pan right side up. Run a long narrow metal spatula around the inside of the cake pan and the tube to release the cake. Remove the sides of the cake pan. Gently pull the cake away from the bottom of the pan and transfer to a serving plate.

**7.** Using a large serrated knife, cut into wedges and serve.

# carrot cake with cream cheese frosting

Our reduced-sugar carrot cake is loaded with such goodies as crushed pineapple and coconut to ensure a delectably moist layer cake. In fact, it is so tasty that you may choose to serve it unfrosted, but if you do prefer an iced cake, know that the cream-cheese frosting used is low-fat.

Nonstick cooking spray and flour
  for the pans

2 cups all-purpose flour

2½ teaspoons ground cinnamon

1½ teaspoons baking powder

1 teaspoon baking soda

1 teaspoon salt

1 cup SPLENDA® Sugar Blend

1 cup vegetable oil

4 large eggs, at room temperature

2¾ cups shredded carrots
  (from about 5 large carrots)

One 8-ounce can crushed pineapple,
  well drained

1 cup sweetened flaked coconut

½ cup chopped walnuts

Cream Cheese Frosting (page 55)

### NUTRITIONAL INFORMATION

Serving Size: 1 slice with frosting
Total Calories: 460
Calories from Fat: 260
Total Fat: 29 g
Saturated Fat: 6.5g
Cholesterol: 80 mg
Sodium: 600 mg
Total Carbohydrates: 44 g
Dietary Fiber: 2 g
Sugars: 22 g
Protein: 9 g

**EXCHANGES PER SERVING**
3 starches, 6 fats

1. Position a rack in the center of the oven and preheat to 325°F. Lightly spray the insides of two 8-inch round cake pans with the cooking spray. Dust the insides of the pans with flour and tap out the excess flour.

2. Sift together the flour, cinnamon, baking powder, baking soda, and salt into a medium bowl. Beat the SPLENDA® Sugar Blend, oil, and eggs in a large bowl with an electric mixer on medium speed until blended. Reduce the speed to low and gradually beat in the flour mixture until smooth, scraping down the sides of the bowl as needed. Stir in the carrots, pine-apple, coconut, and walnuts until combined. Divide the batter evenly between the prepared pans and smooth the tops.

3. Bake until a wooden toothpick inserted in the centers of the cakes comes out clean, 35 to 40 minutes. Let cool on wire racks for 10 minutes. Invert the cakes onto the racks and remove the pans. Turn the cakes right side up and let cool completely.

4. To frost the cake, turn one layer upside down on a serving plate. Spread with about ½ cup of the frosting. Top with the second layer, right side up. Spread the remaining frosting on the top and sides of the cake. Cut into wedges and serve.

# classic chocolate cake

Chocolate cake—moist, sweet, and intense with deep chocolate flavor—is probably at the top of the list of favorite birthday cakes. And when spirits need lifting, nothing beats a slice of this American classic with a cold glass of milk. The coffee in the recipe enhances the chocolate without adding flavor of its own. Ice the cake with the chocolate frosting, or use nonfat whipped topping.

**Nonstick cooking spray and flour for the pans**

**2½ cups all-purpose flour**

**1¼ cups unsweetened cocoa powder**

**1 teaspoon baking powder**

**1 teaspoon baking soda**

**¾ cup (1½ sticks) unsalted butter, at room temperature**

**1¼ cups SPLENDA® Sugar Blend**

**3 large eggs, at room temperature**

**1 teaspoon vanilla extract**

**1½ cups 2% reduced-fat milk**

**¼ cup cold brewed coffee or water**

**Creamy Chocolate Frosting (page 56)**

### NUTRITIONAL INFORMATION

Serving Size: 1 slice with frosting
Total Calories: 430
Calories from Fat: 190
Total Fat: 21 g
Saturated Fat: 13 g
Cholesterol: 85 mg
Sodium: 200 mg
Total Carbohydrates: 57 g
Dietary Fiber: 3 g
Sugars: 33 g
Protein: 7 g

EXCHANGES PER SERVING
4 starches, 4 fats

1. Position a rack in the center of the oven and preheat the oven to 350°F. Lightly spray the insides of two 8-inch round cake pans with the cooking spray. Dust the insides of the pans with flour and tap out the excess flour.

2. Sift together the flour, cocoa powder, baking powder, and baking soda into a medium bowl. Beat the butter in a large bowl with an electric mixer on high speed until creamy, about 1 minute. Gradually beat in the SPLENDA® Sugar Blend. Add the eggs, one at a time, beating well after each addition. Beat in the vanilla.

3. Reduce the speed to low and beat in half of the flour mixture. Beat in the milk and coffee. Add the remaining flour mixture and beat until smooth, scraping down the sides of the bowl as needed. Divide the batter evenly between the prepared pans and smooth the tops.

4. Bake until a wooden toothpick inserted in the centers of the cakes comes out clean, 35 to 40 minutes. Let cool on wire racks for 10 minutes. Invert the cakes onto the wire racks, remove the pans, and let cool completely.

5. To frost the cake, turn one layer upside down on a serving plate. Spread with about ½ cup of the frosting. Top with the second layer, right side up. Spread the remaining frosting on the top and sides of the cake. Cut into wedges and serve.

# chocolate cupcakes

Tucked into a lunch box (and not necessarily just kids' lunch boxes), delivered to a bake sale, shared with coworkers, or baked up to celebrate good times, a chocolate cupcake will always bring a smile. This recipe makes a large batch, so unless you plan on sharing with others, make room in your freezer to store leftovers. Frost with Creamy Chocolate Frosting (page 56) if you wish.

½ cup unsweetened cocoa powder

½ cup boiling water

1½ cups sifted cake flour
   (sifted first, then measured)

½ teaspoon baking soda

¼ teaspoon salt

1 cup SPLENDA® Sugar Blend

¾ cup (1½ sticks) unsalted butter,
   thinly sliced, at room temperature

2 large eggs, at room temperature

¼ cup whole milk

1 teaspoon vanilla extract

Confectioners' sugar (or "Powdered Sugar,"
   see page 36) for garnish or Creamy
   Chocolate Frosting (page 56), optional

### NUTRITIONAL INFORMATION

Serving Size: 1 cupcake
   without garnish or
   frosting
Total Calories: 160
Calories from Fat: 80
Total Fat: 9 g
Saturated Fat: 5 g
Cholesterol: 45 mg

Sodium: 80 mg
Total Carbohydrates: 20 g
Dietary Fiber: 1 g
Sugars: 11 g
Protein: 2 g

EXCHANGES PER SERVING
1½ starches, 1 fat

1. Position a rack in the center of the oven and preheat to 350°F. Line 18 muffin cups with foil liners.

2. Whisk the cocoa powder and boiling water in a small bowl until the cocoa dissolves. Sift together the flour, baking soda, and salt into a large bowl. Stir in the SPLENDA® Sugar Blend. Add the butter. Using a pastry blender, two knives, or an electric mixer on low speed, cut the butter into the flour mixture until the mixture is uniformly crumbly.

3. Whisk the eggs, milk, and vanilla in a bowl until well blended. Beat in the cocoa mixture. Using an electric mixer on low speed, add one-third of the milk mixture to the bowl with the flour mixture and beat until the batter is just smooth, scraping down the sides of the bowl as needed. Repeat twice with the remaining milk mixture. Divide the batter evenly among the muffin cups.

4. Bake until a wooden toothpick inserted in the center of a cupcake comes out clean, about 22 minutes. Let cool for 5 minutes in the pan on a wire rack. Remove the cupcakes in their liners from the pan and let cool completely on the rack.

5. Sift confectioners' sugar over the top of the cupcakes or frost with the chocolate frosting, if desired.

# banana-hazelnut cake

Toasted hazelnuts add a touch of European sophistication to this fine dessert, but that's far from its only attribute: The sugar, fat, and calories of the traditional recipe have been substantially reduced. Cake flour, which has a low gluten content, will make a tender cake. Be sure to use very ripe bananas—the peels should be freckled all over with brown spots, but not entirely black.

**Nonstick cooking spray for the pan**

**1 cup (4 oz) hazelnuts**

**3¼ cups cake flour**

**2½ teaspoons baking powder**

**1 teaspoon baking soda**

**½ cup nonfat dry milk powder**

**2 cups mashed very ripe bananas (about 5 large bananas)**

**1⅓ cups SPLENDA® No Calorie Sweetener, Granulated**

**1 cup low-fat buttermilk**

**½ cup liquid egg substitute**

**½ cup canola or hazelnut oil (see Note)**

**¼ cup firmly packed SPLENDA® Brown Sugar Blend**

**1 tablespoon vanilla extract**

1. Position a rack in the center of the oven and preheat to 350°F. Lightly spray the inside of a 12-cup nonstick fluted tube pan with the cooking spray.

2. Spread the hazelnuts on a rimmed baking sheet. Bake, occasionally stirring them, until the skins are cracked and peeling, about 10 minutes. Transfer the nuts to a kitchen towel and wrap them in the towel. Let stand for 10 minutes. Rub the nuts in the towel to remove as much of the skins as possible. Coarsely chop the nuts and set aside.

3. Sift together the flour, baking powder, and baking soda in a medium bowl. Stir in the dry milk. Combine the bananas, SPLENDA® Granulated Sweetener, buttermilk, egg substitute, oil, SPLENDA® Brown Sugar Blend, and vanilla in a large bowl and mix well. Add the flour mixture and stir well until combined. Fold in the nuts. Spread the batter evenly in the prepared pan.

4. Bake until a wooden toothpick inserted in the center of the cake comes out clean, about 1 hour. Let cool on a wire rack for 10 minutes. Invert the cake onto the rack, remove the pan, and let cool completely.

5. Cut into wedges and serve.

**NOTE:** For an even deeper nutty flavor, use hazelnut oil, available at specialty markets and well-stocked supermarkets.

### NUTRITIONAL INFORMATION

| | |
|---|---|
| Serving Size: 1 slice | Sodium: 150 mg |
| Total Calories: 220 | Total Carbohydrates: 29 g |
| Calories from Fat: 90 | Dietary Fiber: 2 g |
| Total Fat: 10 g | Sugars: 7 g |
| Saturated Fat: 1 g | Protein: 5 g |
| Cholesterol: 0 mg | **EXCHANGES PER SERVING** |
| | 2 starches, 2 fats |

# lemon velvet layer cake

Tender cake layers combined with a luscious lemon filling make this a special occasion cake par excellence. It would be perfect served with citrus-scented tea at an elegant luncheon. To gild the lily, spread the tops and sides with the whipped cream frosting.

### Cake

**Nonstick cooking spray and all-purpose flour for the pans**

**2½ cups sifted cake flour (sifted first, then measured)**

**1 cup SPLENDA® Sugar Blend**

**2½ teaspoons baking powder**

**½ teaspoon salt**

**½ cup (1 stick) unsalted butter, thinly sliced, at room temperature**

**3 large eggs**

**1 cup whole milk**

**1 teaspoon grated lemon zest**

**¼ teaspoon lemon extract**

1. Position a rack in the center of the oven and preheat to 350°F. Lightly spray the insides of two 8-inch round cake pans with the cooking spray. Dust the insides of the pans with all-purpose flour and tap out the excess flour.

2. To make the cake layers, sift together the cake flour, SPLENDA® Sugar Blend, baking powder, and salt into a large bowl. Add the butter. Using a pastry blender, two knives, or an electric mixer on low speed, cut the butter into the flour mixture until the mixture is uniformly crumbly.

3. Whisk the eggs, milk, lemon zest, and lemon extract in a bowl until well blended. Using an electric mixer on low speed, add one-third of the milk mixture to the bowl with the flour mixture and beat until the batter is smooth, about 30 seconds, scraping down the sides of the bowl as needed. Repeat twice with the remaining milk mixture. Divide the batter evenly between the prepared pans and smooth the tops.

4. Bake until a wooden toothpick inserted in the centers of the cakes comes out clean, 25 to 30 minutes. Let cool on wire racks for 10 minutes. Invert the cakes onto the racks, remove the pans, and let cool completely.

## Lemon Filling

⅔ cup SPLENDA® Sugar Blend

2½ tablespoons cornstarch

1 cup water

2 large egg yolks, lightly beaten

¼ cup fresh lemon juice

2 tablespoons grated lemon zest

2 tablespoons unsalted butter

## Whipped Cream Frosting

1¼ cups heavy cream

2 tablespoons SPLENDA® Sugar Blend

1 teaspoon grated lemon zest

¼ teaspoon lemon extract

### NUTRITIONAL INFORMATION

Serving Size: 1 slice with whipped cream frosting

Total Calories: 310

Calories from Fat: 150

Total Fat: 16 g

Saturated Fat: 10 g

Cholesterol: 110 mg

Sodium: 170 mg

Total Carbohydrates: 40 g

Dietary Fiber: 1 g

Sugars: 24 g

Protein: 4 g

EXCHANGES PER SERVING

2½ starches, 3 fats

5. To make the filling: Combine the SPLENDA® Sugar Blend and cornstarch in a medium saucepan. Gradually whisk in the water to dissolve the cornstarch. Whisking constantly, bring to a boil over medium heat. Meanwhile, beat the egg yolks in a small bowl. Whisk about one-fourth of the hot cornstarch mixture into the yolks, stir well, and return this mixture to the saucepan. Cook, whisking constantly, until the mixture returns to a boil. Reduce the heat to medium-low and cook for 1 minute. Remove from the heat and stir in the lemon juice and zest and the butter. Transfer to a small bowl. Place a piece of waxed paper or plastic wrap directly on the surface of the filling to prevent a skin from forming. Poke a few holes in the plastic wrap with the tip of a small knife. Let the filling cool completely.

6. To make the frosting, beat the heavy cream in a medium bowl with an electric mixer on high speed until the cream is foamy. Add the SPLENDA® Sugar Blend, grated lemon zest, and lemon extract and beat until soft peaks form. Use immediately.

7. To assemble the cake, turn one layer upside down on a serving plate. Spread with the filling. Top with the second layer, right side up. Spread the whipped cream frosting on the top and sides of the cake, if desired. Cut into wedges and serve.

Fluted tube pans, also called Bundt pans, can be used in place of standard cake pans for many of these cakes to give them a more decorative or festive shape. A classic tube pan holds 12 cups; some of the newer designs hold 10 cups. To check your pan's capacity, fill it with cups of water. No matter the size of the cake pan, fill it only two-thirds with batter to allow for rising.

# yellow cupcakes with creamy chocolate frosting

What is it about a cupcake that gives it so much charm? It could be its diminutive size, or that it makes a single handheld serving to savor one bite at a time. Or perhaps it brings back memories of a simpler time. Yellow cupcakes with chocolate frosting are a classic of the genre, offered here in a reduced-calorie version. For the traditional decoration, top the frosting with colored sprinkles.

*sugar blend*

**Nonstick cooking spray for the liners**

**1½ cups cake flour**

**1 teaspoon baking powder**

**¼ teaspoon baking soda**

**½ cup SPLENDA® Sugar Blend**

**5 tablespoons unsalted butter,
 at room temperature**

**⅔ cup low-fat buttermilk**

**½ cup liquid egg substitute**

**1 teaspoon vanilla extract**

**Creamy Chocolate Frosting (page 56),
 optional**

### NUTRITIONAL INFORMATION

Serving Size: 1 cupcake
 without frosting
Total Calories: 150
Calories from Fat: 45
Total Fat: 5 g
Saturated Fat: 3.5 g
Cholesterol: 15 mg

Sodium: 95 mg
Total Carbohydrates: 23 g
Dietary Fiber: 0 g
Sugars: 9 g
Protein: 3 g
**EXCHANGES PER SERVING**
1½ starches, 1 fat

Serving Size: 1 cupcake
 with frosting
Total Calories: 330
Calories from Fat: 140
Total Fat: 16 g
Saturated Fat: 10 g
Cholesterol: 35 mg

Sodium: 105 mg
Total Carbohydrates: 44 g
Dietary Fiber: 1 g
Sugars: 26 g
Protein: 4 g
**EXCHANGES PER SERVING**
3 starches, 3 fats

1. Position a rack in the center of the oven and preheat to 350°F. Line 12 muffin cups with paper or foil liners (see page 62). Lightly spray liners with the cooking spray.

2. Sift together the flour, baking powder, and baking soda into a large bowl. Stir in the SPLENDA® Sugar Blend. Add the butter. Using a pastry blender, two knives, or an electric mixer on low speed, cut the butter into the flour mixture until the mixture is uniformly crumbly. Whisk the buttermilk, egg substitute, and vanilla in a bowl until well blended. Using an electric mixer on low speed, add the buttermilk mixture to the bowl with the flour mixture and beat until the batter is smooth, about 30 seconds, scraping down the sides of the bowl as needed. Divide the batter evenly among the muffin cups.

3. Bake until a wooden toothpick inserted in the center of a cupcake comes out clean, about 18 minutes. Let cool for 5 minutes in the pan on a wire rack. Remove the cupcakes in their liners from the pan and let cool completely on the rack.

4. Spread the chocolate frosting on the cupcakes, if desired.

# polka-dot cake

Here is a celebratory cake that will make any party a special occasion. The tender, golden yellow cake is spread with creamy frosting and decked out in colorful meringue dots. To give the dots the most vivid colors, use paste or gel food coloring, available at kitchenware or craft shops.

## Meringue Dots

⅓ cup warm (105° to 115°F) water, or more as needed

2 tablespoons meringue powder (see Note, page 175)

2¼ cups SPLENDA® No Calorie Sweetener, Granulated

⅓ cup plus 1 tablespoon cornstarch

½ teaspoon cream of tartar

½ teaspoon vanilla extract

Liquid gel or paste food coloring (optional)

> CONTINUED

1. To make the meringue dots, position a rack in the center of the oven and preheat to 250°F. Line a large baking sheet with waxed paper.

2. Whisk the ⅓ cup warm water and meringue powder together in a medium bowl until the powder is dissolved. Let stand for 3 minutes. Meanwhile, in a food processor, combine the SPLENDA® Granulated Sweetener, cornstarch, and cream of tartar and process until ground into a very fine powder, about 30 seconds. Add half of the SPLENDA® mixture and the vanilla to the meringue powder mixture. Using an electric mixer on medium speed, beat until combined. Add the remaining SPLENDA® mixture and beat on high speed until the meringue is very stiff, about 5 minutes. The meringue should be stiff but soft enough to pipe; add a bit more water if needed.

3. Tint the meringue with food coloring as desired; leave plain for white dots. If you want dots of different colors, divide the meringue among small bowls and color each separately. Be sparing at first with the coloring; you can always add more. The meringue dries quickly, so keep each portion covered with a damp paper towel as you work. Transfer the meringue to a pastry bag fitted with a plain ¼-inch tip (if you make more than one color, use a separate pastry bag for each). Pipe about forty-eight 1-inch-wide rounds onto the prepared baking sheet. Leave small peaks or smooth the tops with a finger dipped in water as you like; a combination of the two creates a nice visual appeal. Bake the meringues until crisp, about 30 minutes. Let cool for 5 minutes, then use a thin spatula to transfer them to a clean piece of waxed paper or baking sheet and let cool completely.

> CONTINUED

## Cake

**Nonstick cooking spray and all-purpose flour for the pans**

**3 cups cake flour**

**2 teaspoons baking powder**

**½ teaspoon baking soda**

**1 cup SPLENDA® Sugar Blend**

**¾ cup (1½ sticks) unsalted butter, cut into 12 slices, at room temperature**

**1¼ cups low-fat buttermilk**

**4 large egg yolks**

**2 teaspoons vanilla extract**

**Cream Cheese Frosting (facing page)**

### NUTRITIONAL INFORMATION

Serving Size: 3 Polka Dots
Total Calories: 30
Calories from Fat: 0
Total Fat: 0 g
Saturated Fat: 0 g
Cholesterol: 0 mg
Sodium: 10 mg

Total Carbohydrates: 6 g
Dietary Fiber: 0 g
Sugars: 0 g
Protein: 1 g
**EXCHANGES PER SERVING**
½ starches

Serving Size: 1 slice Polka-Dot Cake with Cream Cheese Frosting and 3 "dots"
Total Calories: 330
Calories from Fat: 120
Total Fat: 13 g
Saturated Fat: 8 g
Cholesterol: 85 mg

Sodium: 290 mg
Total Carbohydrates: 45 g
Dietary Fiber: 0 g
Sugars: 15 g
Protein: 9 g
**EXCHANGES PER SERVING**
3 starches, 2 fats

4. To make the cake layers, raise the oven temperature to 350°F. Lightly spray the insides of two 8-inch round cake pans with the cooking spray. Dust the insides of the pans with all-purpose flour and tap out the excess flour.

5. Sift together the cake flour, baking powder, and baking soda into a large bowl. Whisk in the SPLENDA® Sugar Blend. Add the butter. Using an electric mixer on low speed, cut the butter into the flour mixture until the mixture is uniformly crumbly, about 1 minute.

6. Whisk the buttermilk, egg yolks, and vanilla together in a small bowl. Add half of the buttermilk mixture to the flour mixture and beat on medium-high speed, scraping down the sides of the bowl often, until smooth and blended, about 45 seconds. Add the remaining buttermilk mixture and beat until mixed well, scraping down the bowl as needed. Divide the batter evenly between the prepared pans and smooth the tops.

7. Bake until a wooden toothpick inserted in the centers of the cakes comes out clean, about 35 minutes. Let cool on wire racks for 10 minutes. Invert the cakes onto the wire racks, remove the pans, and let cool completely.

8. To assemble the cake, turn one layer upside down on a serving plate. Spread with a thin layer of the frosting. Top with the second layer, right side up. Spread the remaining frosting on the top and sides of the cake. Decorate with the meringue dots. Cut into wedges and serve.

# cream cheese frosting

This smooth-as-silk frosting is most classically used to ice Carrot Cake (page 43), but it is equally fine as a topping for Chocolate Cupcakes (page 46). Many of the calories and fat grams found in other recipes have been reduced, so you can use it without guilt. Just be sure that the cream cheese is well softened—let it stand at room temperature for an hour or two before making the frosting.

**1 pound nonfat cream cheese,**
**well softened**

**1 cup SPLENDA® No Calorie Sweetener,**
**Granulated**

**½ cup (1 stick) light butter,**
**at room temperature**

**2 teaspoons vanilla extract**

### NUTRITIONAL INFORMATION

Serving Size:
  2 tablespoons
Total Calories: 60
Calories from Fat: 30
Total Fat: 3 g
Saturated Fat: 2 g
Cholesterol: 10 mg

Sodium: 190 mg
Total Carbohydrates: 3 g
Dietary Fiber: 0 g
Sugars: 0 g
Protein: 3 g

**EXCHANGES PER SERVING**
1 fat

1. Cut the cream cheese into chunks and place in a bowl. Let stand at room temperature until it is very soft, at least 1 and up to 2 hours.

2. Beat the SPLENDA® Granulated Sweetener and butter in a medium bowl with an electric mixer on medium speed just until blended. Do not overbeat. One tablespoon at a time, beat in the cream cheese, scraping down the sides of the bowl as needed, until smooth. Beat in the vanilla. If the frosting seems too soft to spread, cover and refrigerate until firmer.

When a recipe calls for butter at room temperature, let it soften just until the butter holds an impression when pressed, but is still somewhat cool and not shiny or squishy. The butter must be malleable enough to allow air to be beaten into it, but very soft butter will not support the tiny, invisible air bubbles. If you need to speed the softening along in a microwave, cut the butter into chunks, place in a microwave-safe bowl, and microwave on Low in ten-second intervals just until it reaches the right consistency.

# creamy chocolate frosting

This is the chocolate frosting to turn to when you need a sweet finish to your chocolate cake or cupcakes. Old-time cookbooks call this a "boiled frosting," as it is cooked on the stove top and then cooled to spreading consistency. It is a time-tested, reliable icing that will very likely become a favorite.

1 cup SPLENDA® Sugar Blend

⅓ cup all-purpose flour

¾ cup 2% reduced-fat milk

2 ounces unsweetened chocolate, coarsely chopped

½ cup (1 stick) unsalted butter, thinly sliced, at room temperature

1½ teaspoons vanilla extract

### NUTRITIONAL INFORMATION

Serving Size: 2 tablespoons
Total Calories: 180
Calories from Fat: 90
Total Fat: 10 g
Saturated Fat: 7 g
Cholesterol: 20 mg

Sodium: 10 mg
Total Carbohydrates: 23 g
Dietary Fiber: 1 g
Sugars: 19 g
Protein: 2 g

EXCHANGES PER SERVING
1½ starches, 2 fats

1. Combine the SPLENDA® Sugar Blend and flour in a heavy-bottomed medium saucepan. Gradually whisk in the milk until the mixture is smooth. Cook over medium-heat heat, whisking constantly, until the mixture comes to a boil. Reduce the heat to low and simmer, whisking often, until the mixture has a pudding-like consistency, about 5 minutes.

2. Remove from the heat and add the chocolate. Let stand for 2 minutes, then whisk until the chocolate melts. Add the butter and whisk until it is incorporated. Transfer the frosting to a medium bowl.

3. Place the bowl in a larger bowl of iced water. Let stand, stirring occasionally with a rubber spatula, until the frosting is cool and thick enough to spread, 10 to 20 minutes. Stir in the vanilla.

quick breads, muffins,
and coffee cakes

# applesauce snacking cake

When you need a tasty sweet to brighten the day—one that can be made in almost no time and quickly baked, and is equally mouthwatering served warm from the pan or cooled off—this spicy applesauce cake is the answer. This recipe is reduced in calories, fat, and sugar content, but is still full of old-fashioned goodness. Dust the top with confectioners' sugar, if you like.

**Nonstick cooking spray for the pan**

**1 cup all-purpose flour**

**1 teaspoon baking powder**

**½ teaspoon baking soda**

**2 teaspoons ground cinnamon**

**½ teaspoon ground ginger**

**½ cup (1 stick) reduced-calorie margarine**

**¼ cup unsulfured molasses**

**½ cup liquid egg substitute**

**1 teaspoon vanilla extract**

**1 cup SPLENDA® No Calorie Sweetener, Granulated**

**½ cup unsweetened applesauce**

1. Position a rack in the center of the oven and preheat to 350°F. Lightly spray the inside of an 8-inch square baking pan with the cooking spray.

2. Sift the together flour, baking powder, baking soda, cinnamon, and ginger into a bowl. Beat the margarine and molasses in a large bowl with an electric mixer on high speed until well combined, about 1 minute. Add the egg substitute and vanilla and beat for 30 seconds; the mixture will be very liquid. Gradually add the SPLENDA® Granulated Sweetener, then beat until the mixture is very smooth, about 1½ minutes. Reduce the speed to low, add the flour mixture and applesauce, and beat until smooth, scraping down the sides of the bowl as needed. Spread the batter evenly in the prepared pan.

3. Bake until the top springs back when pressed in the center, about 30 minutes. Let cool in the pan on a wire rack for 10 minutes. Cut into squares and serve warm, or cool to room temperature and then cut and serve.

### NUTRITIONAL INFORMATION

Serving Size: 1 square
Total Calories: 170
Calories from Fat: 60
Total Fat: 6 g
Saturated Fat: 1 g
Cholesterol: 0 mg

Sodium: 310 mg
Total Carbohydrates: 24 g
Dietary Fiber: 1 g
Sugars: 6 g
Protein: 4 g

**EXCHANGES PER SERVING**
1½ starches, 1 fat

# banana-walnut bread

This banana bread is good for you in many ways. The bananas supply potassium and dietary fiber, and you'll get omega-3 fatty acids from the walnuts. What you won't get is a lot of cholesterol, as canola oil and buttermilk stand in for butter. Good banana bread starts with well-ripened bananas, so hold off making this until your fruit is freckled all over—but not black, as black bananas give baked goods an "off" taste.

**Nonstick cooking spray for the pan**

**1⅓ cups all-purpose flour**

**1 teaspoon baking powder**

**½ teaspoon baking soda**

**Pinch of salt**

**½ cup SPLENDA® No Calorie Sweetener, Granulated**

**1¼ cups very ripe, mashed bananas (from about 4 large bananas)**

**⅓ cup low-fat buttermilk**

**1 tablespoon canola oil**

**2 teaspoons vanilla extract**

**¼ cup chopped walnuts**

1. Position a rack in the center of the oven and preheat to 350°F. Lightly spray the inside of an 8½-by-4½-inch loaf pan with the cooking spray.

2. Sift together the flour, baking powder, baking soda, and salt into a medium bowl. Add in the SPLENDA® Granulated Sweetener. Combine the bananas, buttermilk, oil, and vanilla in another bowl and mix well, then add to the flour mixture. Stir just until combined. Stir in the walnuts. Spread the batter evenly in the prepared pan.

3. Bake until a wooden toothpick inserted in the center of the loaf comes out clean, 45 to 55 minutes. Let cool in the pan for 10 minutes on a wire rack. Invert the loaf onto the rack, remove the pan, and let cool completely. Cut into slices and serve.

### NUTRITIONAL INFORMATION

Serving Size: 1 slice
Total Calories: 170
Calories from Fat: 50
Total Fat: 5 g
Saturated Fat: 0.5 g
Cholesterol: 0 mg

Sodium: 180 mg
Total Carbohydrates: 27 g
Dietary Fiber: 2 g
Sugars: 5 g
Protein: 4 g

**EXCHANGES PER SERVING**
1 starch, 1 fruit, 1 fat

Many of these baked goods are perfect breakfast or brunch fare. To speed making doughs and batters in the morning, prepare the ingredients the night before. Measure out all of the ingredients—dry ingredients can be kept covered at room temperature, but refrigerate appropriate dairy products and eggs. On the next day, it's just a question of whipping things together while the oven preheats.

# blueberry-almond coffee cake

This irresistible coffee cake is liberally studded with blueberries and crowned with a crunchy, glazed-almond topping. The only problem you'll have is deciding when to serve it—breakfast or brunch, an afternoon gathering, or as an easy dessert for dinner.

### Cake

**Nonstick cooking spray for the pan**

**2 cups all-purpose flour**

**2 teaspoons baking powder**

**¾ teaspoon salt**

**½ cup (1 stick) unsalted butter**

**1 cup SPLENDA® No Calorie Sweetener, Granulated**

**2 large eggs, at room temperature**

**1 teaspoon vanilla extract**

**¼ teaspoon almond extract**

**½ cup 1% low-fat milk**

**1½ cups fresh or unthawed frozen blueberries**

### Topping

**1 large egg white**

**¾ cup sliced almonds**

**3 tablespoons SPLENDA® No Calorie Sweetener, Granulated**

1. Position a rack in the center of the oven and preheat to 350°F. Lightly spray the inside of an 8-inch square baking pan with the spray.

2. To make the cake, sift together the flour, baking powder, and salt into a bowl. Beat the softened butter in a large bowl with an electric mixer on high speed until creamy, about 1 minute. Gradually beat in the SPLENDA® Granulated Sweetener and beat until the mixture is light in color and texture, about 3 minutes. One at a time, beat in the eggs, mixing well after each addition. Add the vanilla and almond extracts. Reduce the speed to low and beat in three additions of the flour mixture, alternating with two additions of the milk, beating until smooth after each addition and scraping down the sides of the bowl as needed. Stir in the blueberries. Spread the batter evenly in the prepared pan.

3. To make the topping, beat the egg white in a small bowl with a fork until foamy. Add the almonds and SPLENDA® Granulated Sweetener and mix until the almonds are coated. Spoon the almond mixture evenly over the batter.

4. Bake until a wooden toothpick inserted in the center of the cake comes out clean, 50 to 60 minutes. Let cool in the pan on a wire rack for 10 minutes. Serve warm, or let cool to room temperature. Cut into squares and serve.

### NUTRITIONAL INFORMATION

| | |
|---|---|
| Serving Size: 1 square | Sodium: 250 mg |
| Total Calories: 220 | Total Carbohydrates: 23 g |
| Calories from Fat: 110 | Dietary Fiber: 2 g |
| Total Fat: 12 g | Sugars: 3 g |
| Saturated Fat: 5 g | Protein: 5 g |
| Cholesterol: 55 mg | Exchanges per serving |
| | 1½ starches, 2 fats |

# blueberry muffins

Start the day in a sweet way with these excellent muffins, bursting with summery blueberries and with a tender, cakelike texture. Although the muffins are much lighter than the traditional recipe, no one will ever know the difference. However, do expect them to be a bit paler than old-fashioned versions. If you use frozen berries, add them unthawed to the batter, or they will tint the muffins purple.

2 cups all-purpose flour

2 teaspoons baking powder

¾ teaspoon salt

½ cup (1 stick) light margarine

1 cup SPLENDA® No Calorie Sweetener, Granulated

¼ cup honey

2 large eggs, at room temperature

1 teaspoon vanilla extract

½ cup 1% low-fat milk

1 cup fresh or unthawed frozen blueberries

### NUTRITIONAL INFORMATION

Serving Size: 1 muffin
Total Calories: 160
Calories from Fat: 40
Total Fat: 4.5 g
Saturated Fat: 1 g
Cholesterol: 35 mg

Sodium: 230 mg
Total Carbohydrates: 26 g
Dietary Fiber: 1 g
Sugars: 7 g
Protein: 4 g

**EXCHANGES PER SERVING**
1½ starches, 1 fat

1. Position a rack in the center of the oven and preheat to 350°F. Line 12 muffin cups with foil liners.

2. Sift together the flour, baking powder, and salt into a bowl. Beat the margarine in a large bowl with an electric mixer on high speed until creamy, about 1 minute. Gradually beat in the SPLENDA® Granulated Sweetener and honey—do not worry if the mixture separates. One at a time, beat in the eggs, mixing well after each addition—the mixture will come together. Add the vanilla. Reduce the speed to low and beat in three additions of the flour mixture, alternating with two additions of the milk, beating until smooth after each addition and scraping the sides of the bowl as needed. Stir in the blueberries. Spoon equal amounts of the batter into the muffin cups.

3. Bake until a wooden toothpick inserted in the center of a muffin comes out clean, 25 to 30 minutes. Let cool in the pan on a wire rack for 5 minutes. Remove the muffins in their liners from the pan and serve warm, or let cool completely on the rack.

Foil liners for muffins are non-stick and make for easy removal from muffin pans. If you prefer to use paper liners, spray the insides of the liners with non-stick cooking spray.

# caramel sticky buns

Your loved ones will wake up with a smile when served a freshly baked batch of these wonderful rolls at breakfast time. The dough rises overnight, so there isn't a lot of work involved in the morning. Bake off all three pans of rolls and freeze some for another morning.

### Dough

1 cup water

½ cup (1 stick) unsalted butter, thinly sliced, at room temperature

One ¼-ounce envelope (2¼ teaspoons) active dry yeast (see Note, page 64)

½ cup warm (105° to 115°F) water

2 large eggs, at room temperature

¼ cup SPLENDA® Sugar Blend

1¼ teaspoons salt

About 5 cups all-purpose flour, as needed

Canola oil for the bowl

> CONTINUED

1. To make the dough, bring the water to a boil in a small saucepan over high heat. Remove from the heat and add the butter. Stir until the butter melts. Let stand until the mixture cools to lukewarm (no warmer than 105°F), about 20 minutes.

2. Sprinkle the yeast over the warm water in a small bowl. Let stand for 5 minutes, then stir to dissolve.

3. Beat the eggs in the bowl of a standing heavy-duty mixer fitted with the paddle blade on medium speed. Beat in the SPLENDA® Sugar Blend and salt, then the dissolved yeast and the cooled butter mixture. Reduce the speed to low and add the flour, 1 cup at a time, until a soft, slightly sticky dough forms. (Alternatively, beat the eggs, SPLENDA® Sugar Blend, and salt in a large bowl. Add the dissolved yeast and cooled butter mixture. Using a sturdy spoon, stir in enough of the flour to make a dough.)

4. Change to the dough hook and knead the dough in the bowl until the dough is smooth and supple, about 10 minutes. (Or turn the dough out onto a lightly floured work surface and knead by hand, adding just enough flour as needed to keep the dough from sticking to your hands.) The dough will remain slightly sticky.

5. Oil a large bowl. Gather the dough into a ball, roll in the bowl to coat with oil, then settle the dough smooth side up in the bowl. Cover with plastic wrap and refrigerate until the dough has doubled in volume and is chilled, at least 8 hours or overnight.

> CONTINUED

### Caramel Sauce

Canola oil for the pans

¾ cup firmly packed SPLENDA® Brown Sugar Blend

5 tablespoons unsalted butter

3 tablespoons 2% reduced-fat milk

2 tablespoons light corn syrup

1 cup chopped pecans, divided

### Assembly

4 tablespoons unsalted butter, melted

1 cup firmly packed SPLENDA® Brown Sugar Blend

1 teaspoon ground cinnamon

NUTRITIONAL INFORMATION

Serving Size: 1 bun
Total Calories: 220
Calories from Fat: 70
Total Fat: 8 g
Saturated Fat: 5 g
Cholesterol: 35 mg

Sodium: 120 mg
Total Carbohydrates: 34 g
Dietary Fiber: 1 g
Sugars: 16 g
Protein: 3 g
EXCHANGES PER SERVING
2 starches, 1 fat

6. To make the caramel sauce, lightly oil three 8-inch round cake pans (aluminum foil pans are fine). Combine the SPLENDA® Brown Sugar Blend, butter, milk, and corn syrup in a medium saucepan. Stir constantly over low heat until the SPLENDA® dissolves. Raise the heat to high and boil (watch out for boiling over) until slightly thickened, about 1 minute. Immediately pour equal amounts of the caramel sauce into each pan and tip the pans to coat the bottoms evenly. Sprinkle ⅓ cup pecans evenly in each pan.

7. To assemble the rolls, punch down the dough. Transfer to a clean work surface and cut into three equal portions. Keeping the remaining dough covered with plastic wrap, roll out one portion of dough into a 12-by-10-inch rectangle. Brush the dough with some of the melted butter. Mix the SPLENDA® Brown Sugar Blend and cinnamon in a small bowl. Sprinkle the dough rectangle with one third of the SPLENDA® mixture, leaving a ½-inch border around all sides. Starting at a long end, roll up the dough and pinch closed at the long seam. Cut the dough into 9 slices. Arrange the slices, cut side down, in one of the prepared pans. Repeat with the remaining 2 pieces of dough, melted butter, and SPLENDA® mixture.

8. Cover each pan with plastic wrap and let stand in a warm place until the dough doubles in volume, about 2 hours.

9. Position a rack in the center of the oven and preheat to 375°F. Remove the plastic wrap from the buns and bake until the tops are golden brown, about 20 minutes. Let cool on wire racks for 5 minutes. Invert the rolls from each pan onto a plate and remove the pans. Serve warm.

NOTE: For the best results, check the expiration date on yeast packages and do not use any yeast that has expired.

# dried cherry and almond scones

These golden treats can go from inspiration to serving in 30 minutes. Use this basic recipe to create variations with other dried fruits: cranberries, currants, or apricots (chop the latter first) are all fine stand-ins for the cherries. To make perfectly shaped scones, use a small ice cream scoop (1½-ounce, or 3 tablespoons, capacity) to form the mounds of dough.

**Nonstick cooking spray for the baking sheet**

**1 large egg plus 1 large egg white**

**⅔ cup SPLENDA® No Calorie Sweetener, Granulated**

**½ cup low-fat buttermilk**

**⅓ cup canola oil**

**⅓ cup nonfat dry milk**

**½ teaspoon almond extract**

**2 cups all-purpose flour**

**1 teaspoon baking powder**

**½ teaspoon baking soda**

**1 cup dried cherries, coarsely chopped**

1. Position a rack in the center of the oven and preheat to 350°F. Lightly spray a baking sheet with the cooking spray.

2. Whisk the egg and egg white in a medium bowl until combined. Add the SPLENDA® Granulated Sweetener, buttermilk, oil, dry milk, and almond extract and whisk until mixed. Sift together the flour, baking powder, and baking soda into the bowl and stir just until blended. Stir in the cherries. Spoon 12 equal-sized mounds onto the prepared baking sheet.

3. Bake until the undersides of the scones are golden brown (lift one gently with a spatula to check), 12 to 15 minutes. Serve warm.

When mixing quick breads, scones, and muffins, do not overbeat the batter. Excessive stirring will toughen the gluten in the flour and create air bubbles that make the batter rise unevenly during baking. Stir the batter just until all of the ingredients are moistened.

### NUTRITIONAL INFORMATION

Serving Size: 1 scone
Total Calories: 200
Calories from Fat: 60
Total Fat: 7 g
Saturated Fat: 0.5 g
Cholesterol: 20 mg

Sodium: 125 mg
Total Carbohydrates: 28 g
Dietary Fiber: 2 g
Sugars: 8 g
Protein: 5 g

**EXCHANGES PER SERVING**
2 starches, 1 fat

# peach-berry muffins

Chunks of fresh peaches and sweet berries make these buttery muffins extraordinary. Blueberries are the classic muffin berry, but there's no reason not to try blackberries, raspberries, or huckleberries (strawberries are fine, but they lose color when baked). The muffins are almost as good if you use frozen or canned drained fruit out of season.

2 cups all-purpose flour

1½ teaspoons baking powder

½ teaspoon baking soda

⅔ cup 1% low-fat milk

2 tablespoons low-fat peach or plain yogurt

2 large eggs, at room temperature

1¼ cups SPLENDA® No Calorie Sweetener, Granulated

½ cup (1 stick) unsalted butter, melted

1½ teaspoons vanilla extract

½ cup fresh or unthawed frozen blueberries

⅓ cup diced (½-inch dice) unpeeled fresh peaches (from about ½ large peach)

1. Position a rack in the center of the oven and preheat to 350°F. Line 8 muffin cups with foil liners (see page 62).

2. Sift together the flour, baking powder, and baking soda into a bowl. Mix the milk and yogurt in a small bowl.

3. Beat the eggs and SPLENDA® Granulated Sweetener in a medium bowl with an electric mixer on high speed until the eggs have tripled in volume and are pale yellow, about 5 minutes. Beat in the melted butter and vanilla. Reduce the speed to low and mix in three additions of the flour mixture, alternating with two additions of the milk mixture, beating until smooth after each addition and scraping the sides of the bowl as needed. Stir in the blueberries and peaches. Spoon equal amounts of the batter into the muffin cups.

4. Bake until a wooden toothpick inserted in the center of a muffin comes out clean, 25 to 30 minutes. Let cool in the pan on a wire rack for 5 minutes. Remove the muffins in their liners from the pan and serve warm, or let cool completely on the rack.

### NUTRITIONAL INFORMATION

Serving Size: 1 muffin

Total Calories: 280

Calories from Fat: 120

Total Fat: 13 g

Saturated Fat: 8 g

Cholesterol: 85 mg

Sodium: 190 mg

Total Carbohydrates: 33 g

Dietary Fiber: 1 g

Sugars: 5 g

Protein: 6 g

**EXCHANGES PER SERVING**
2 starches, 3 fats

# quick monkey bread

When you hanker for a kitchen filled with sweet and yeasty aromas from home-baked bread, but don't have the time to make dough from scratch, turn to this recipe.

**Nonstick cooking spray for the pan**

**¼ cup chopped pecans**

**2 tablespoons unsalted butter, plus 3 tablespoons melted**

**¼ cup plus ⅓ cup firmly packed SPLENDA® Brown Sugar Blend, divided**

**½ teaspoon ground cinnamon, divided**

**1½ pounds (18 rolls) frozen roll dough, thawed**

NUTRITIONAL INFORMATION

Serving Size: 1 serving (¹⁄₁₈th recipe)
Total Calories: 280
Calories from Fat: 140
Total Fat: 16 g
Saturated Fat: 6 g
Cholesterol: 15 mg
Sodium: 590 mg
Total Carbohydrates: 32 g
Dietary Fiber: 0 g
Sugars: 11 g
Protein: 4 g
EXCHANGES PER SERVING
2 starches, 3 fats

1. Lightly spray the inside of a 12-cup nonstick fluted tube pan with the cooking spray. Sprinkle the pecans in the bottom of the pan.

2. Combine the 2 tablespoons of butter, ¼ cup SPLENDA® Brown Sugar Blend, and ¼ teaspoon of the cinnamon in a small saucepan. Cook over low heat, stirring constantly, until smooth and blended. Pour over the pecans.

3. Mix the remaining ⅓ cup SPLENDA® and ¼ teaspoon cinnamon in a small bowl. Place the melted butter in another small bowl. Cut each thawed roll in half and form each into a ball. Dip the tops of the balls in the melted butter, and then in the cinnamon mixture. As the balls are dipped, layer them, coated side up, in the prepared pan.

4. Cover the pan with plastic wrap. Let stand at room temperature until the dough has doubled in volume, about 50 minutes. (Alternatively, refrigerate and let the dough rise overnight. Remove from the refrigerator and let stand at room temperature to let the dough lose its chill without rising, about 45 minutes.)

5. Position a rack in the center of the oven and preheat to 350°F. Remove the plastic wrap from the pan and bake the bread until it's golden brown and sounds hollow when lightly tapped, about 30 minutes.

6. Transfer to a wire rack. Loosen the edges of the bread from the pan with the tip of a knife. Let cool in the pan for 5 minutes. Invert the bread onto a serving platter and remove the pan. Serve warm, allowing guests to pull individual portions from the bread.

# chocolate-cherry muffins

Chocolate and cherries are good partners, and these moist, cakelike muffins celebrate their friendship. Be sure to use Dutch-process cocoa, which has been alkalized to create especially dark, chocolaty results. This recipe also shows off how buttermilk gives many baked goods their tender, melt-in-your-mouth texture. If you want to decorate these, mix equal amounts of unsweetened cocoa powder and confectioners' sugar, and sift the mixture over the tops.

**Nonstick cooking spray for the liners**

**½ cup Dutch-process cocoa powder**

**½ cup boiling water**

**1½ cups all-purpose flour**

**1½ teaspoons baking powder**

**½ teaspoon baking soda**

**1¼ cups SPLENDA® No Calorie Sweetener, Granulated**

**2 large eggs, at room temperature**

**½ cup (1 stick) unsalted butter, melted**

**1½ teaspoons vanilla extract**

**⅔ cup low-fat buttermilk**

**½ cup coarsely chopped dried cherries**

**½ cup coarsely chopped walnuts**

### NUTRITIONAL INFORMATION

Serving Size: 1 muffin, without topping
Total Calories: 280
Calories from Fat: 150
Total Fat: 17 g
Saturated Fat: 8 g
Cholesterol: 75 mg

Sodium: 180 mg
Total Carbohydrates: 29 g
Dietary Fiber: 3 g
Sugars: 4 g
Protein: 7 g

**EXCHANGES PER SERVING**
2 starches, 3 fats

1. Position a rack in the center of the oven and preheat to 350°F. Line 9 muffin cups with paper or foil liners (see page 62). Lightly spray liners with the cooking spray.

2. Whisk the cocoa powder and boiling water in a small bowl until smooth. Let cool until lukewarm.

3. Sift together the flour, baking powder, and baking soda into a bowl. Beat the SPLENDA® Granulated Sweetener and eggs in a large bowl with an electric mixer on high speed until the eggs have tripled in volume and are pale yellow, about 5 minutes. Reduce the speed to medium, add the melted butter and vanilla, and beat until well combined, about 1 minute. Reduce the speed to low and beat in the cocoa mixture. Mix in three additions of the flour mixture, alternating with two additions of the buttermilk, beating just until smooth after each addition and scraping down the sides of the bowl as needed. Stir in the cherries and walnuts. Spoon equal amounts of the batter into the muffin cups.

4. Bake until a wooden toothpick inserted in the center of a muffin comes out clean, 20 to 25 minutes. Let cool in the pan on a wire rack for 5 minutes. Remove the muffins in their liners from the pan and serve warm, or let cool completely on the rack.

# pumpkin muffins

Granted, pumpkin desserts are always popular in autumn. But the big squash is rich in vitamin A and potassium, and brimming with dietary fiber—it deserves to be used year-round. Savvy bakers know that pumpkin can provide much of the bulk in baked goods without adding unwanted fat. These spicy muffins show versatile pumpkin at its best.

Nonstick cooking spray for the liners

2 cups all-purpose flour

2 teaspoons baking soda

1½ teaspoons baking powder

2 teaspoons pumpkin pie spice
   (see Note)

1 teaspoon ground cinnamon

¼ teaspoon salt

1 cup canned solid-pack pumpkin

¾ cup SPLENDA® Sugar Blend, plus
   6 teaspoons for topping the muffins

¾ cup low-fat buttermilk

¼ cup canola oil

1 large egg plus 1 large egg white

¾ teaspoon vanilla extract

½ cup raisins

1. Position a rack in the center of the oven and preheat to 350°F. Line 12 muffin cups with paper or foil liners (see page 62). Lightly spray liners with the cooking spray.

2. Sift together the flour, baking soda, baking powder, pumpkin pie spice, cinnamon, and salt into a large bowl. Whisk the pumpkin, ¾ cup SPLENDA® Sugar Blend, buttermilk, oil, egg and egg white, and vanilla until blended in another bowl. Add to the dry ingredients and stir just until moistened. Stir in the raisins. Spoon equal amounts of the batter into the muffin cups. Sprinkle ½ teaspoon of the remaining SPLENDA® over each muffin.

3. Bake until a wooden toothpick inserted in the center of a muffin comes out clean, about 15 minutes. Let cool in the pan on a wire rack for 5 minutes. Remove the muffins in their liners from the pan and serve warm, or let cool completely on the rack.

NOTE: If you don't have pumpkin pie spice, you can make your own from spices in your kitchen: Mix 1 teaspoon ground ginger, ½ teaspoon ground allspice, ¼ teaspoon ground nutmeg, and ¼ teaspoon ground cloves.

### NUTRITIONAL INFORMATION

Serving Size: 1 muffin

Total Calories: 210

Calories from Fat: 50

Total Fat: 6 g

Saturated Fat: 0.5 g

Cholesterol: 20 mg

Sodium: 340 mg

Total Carbohydrates: 38 g

Dietary Fiber: 2 g

Sugars: 19 g

Protein: 4 g

EXCHANGES PER SERVING
2½ starches, 1 fat

# zucchini-walnut bread

In the height of the warm weather growing season, kitchens all over America are busy turning the garden's bumper crop of summer squash into zucchini bread. It may be a great way to use up zucchini, but it is also a scrumptious, moist quick bread that couldn't be easier to make (and freezes well, too). The reduced levels of fat and sugar in this version are new reasons to make this classic.

Nonstick cooking spray for the pan

1½ cups all-purpose flour

1½ teaspoons baking powder

½ teaspoon baking soda

½ teaspoon ground cinnamon

¼ teaspoon salt

1¼ cups SPLENDA® No Calorie Sweetener, Granulated

2 large eggs, at room temperature

½ cup unsweetened applesauce

⅓ cup canola oil

1 teaspoon vanilla extract

1 cup shredded zucchini squash (use the coarse holes on a box grater)

½ cup chopped walnuts

1. Position a rack in the center of the oven and preheat to 350°F. Lightly spray the inside of an 8-by-4-inch loaf pan with the cooking spray.

2. Sift together the flour, baking powder, baking soda, cinnamon, and salt into a bowl. Beat the SPLENDA® Granulated Sweetener and eggs in a large bowl with an electric mixer on high speed until the eggs have tripled in volume and are pale yellow, about 5 minutes. On medium speed, beat in the applesauce, oil, and vanilla. Reduce the speed to low, add the flour mixture, and mix just until blended. Stir in the zucchini and then the walnuts. Spread the batter evenly in the prepared pan.

3. Bake until a wooden toothpick inserted in the center of the loaf comes out clean, about 45 minutes. Let cool in the pan for 10 minutes on a wire rack. Invert the loaf onto the rack and let cool completely. Cut into slices and serve.

### NUTRITIONAL INFORMATION

Serving Size: 1 slice

Total Calories: 170

Calories from Fat: 90

Total Fat: 11 g

Saturated Fat: 1 g

Cholesterol: 35 mg

Sodium: 160 mg

Total Carbohydrates: 17 g

Dietary Fiber: 1 g

Sugars: 1 g

Protein: 4 g

EXCHANGES PER SERVING

1 starch, 2 fats

# cinnamon swirl coffee cake

Many a recipe file includes a card for a cinnamon-scented coffee cake made with plenty of sour cream for extra tenderness. But bakers concerned with more healthful alternatives will trade that recipe for this one, which has a few alterations to substantially lighten the beloved original.

**Nonstick cooking spray for the pan**

**3 cups cake flour**

**1 tablespoon baking powder**

**¾ teaspoon baking soda**

**½ cup (1 stick) unsalted butter,
at room temperature**

**1⅓ cups SPLENDA® No Calorie Sweetener,
Granulated**

**1 large egg, at room temperature**

**2 large egg whites, at room temperature**

**2 teaspoons vanilla extract**

**½ cup unsweetened applesauce**

**1½ cups light sour cream, divided**

**2 tablespoons SPLENDA® Brown
Sugar Blend**

**1 teaspoon ground cinnamon**

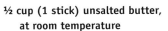

### NUTRITIONAL INFORMATION

Serving Size: 1 slice
Total Calories: 200
Calories from Fat: 70
Total Fat: 8 g
Saturated Fat: 5 g
Cholesterol: 35 mg

Sodium: 180 mg
Total Carbohydrates: 27 g
Dietary Fiber: 1 g
Sugars: 4 g
Protein: 5 g

**EXCHANGES PER SERVING**
2 starches, 1 fat

1. Position a rack in the center of the oven and preheat to 350°F. Lightly spray the inside of a 12-inch tube pan with a fixed bottom (such as an angel food cake pan) or a 10-cup nonstick fluted tube pan with the cooking spray. (A decorative tube pan works beautifully for this recipe.)

2. Sift together the flour, baking powder, and baking soda into a bowl. Beat the butter in a large bowl with an electric mixer on high speed until creamy, about 1 minute. Add the SPLENDA® Granulated Sweetener and the whole egg and beat until combined. Beat in the egg whites and vanilla. On low speed, beat in the applesauce and ¾ cup of the sour cream. Add the flour mixture, raise the speed to medium, and beat just until smooth, scraping down the sides of the bowl as needed. Add the remaining ¾ cup sour cream and beat just until incorporated.

3. Transfer about one-fourth of the batter to a small bowl. Add the SPLENDA® Brown Sugar Blend and cinnamon and mix.

4. Spread half of the remaining plain batter evenly in the prepared pan. Spoon the cinnamon batter over the plain batter. Swirl a knife through the two batters to marbleize them. Top with the remaining plain batter and smooth the top.

5. Bake until a wooden toothpick inserted in the center of the cake comes out clean, 50 to 60 minutes. Let cool on a wire rack for 10 minutes. Invert the cake onto the rack, remove the pan, and let cool completely. Cut into slices and serve.

pies and tarts

# banana cream tart

You *can* indulge in a slice of creamy banana tart from time to time with this reduced-fat version. When cooking pastry cream fillings like this one, let the mixture come to a full boil for at least 1 minute. If not cooked long enough, the filling could break down during chilling, and you'll end up with something like banana soup instead of banana tart.

1 refrigerated prerolled 9-inch piecrust
   dough (half of a 15-ounce package)

*Filling*

¾ cup SPLENDA® No Calorie Sweetener,
   Granulated

¼ cup cornstarch

⅛ teaspoon salt

2 cups 2% reduced-fat milk

⅓ cup liquid egg substitute

1 tablespoon unsalted butter

2 teaspoons vanilla extract

1½ cups sliced bananas
   (about 2 ripe bananas)

Nonfat frozen whipped topping,
   thawed, and finely chopped walnuts
   for garnish (optional)

1. Position a rack in the center of the oven and preheat to 450°F.

2. Unroll the piecrust onto a clean work surface. Fit the piecrust into a 9-inch round tart pan with a removable bottom, being sure that the dough fits tightly where the bottom of the pan meets the sides. Trim the piecrust edges level with the top of the pan. Line the piecrust with aluminum foil, then fill with pie weights or dried beans. Place the pie pan on a baking sheet.

3. Bake until the edges of the crust begin to brown, about 8 minutes. Lift off the foil and weights and continue baking until the crust is lightly browned. Let cool completely in the pan on a wire rack.

4. Meanwhile, make the filling: Mix the SPLENDA® Granulated Sweetener, cornstarch, and salt in a heavy-bottomed medium saucepan. Gradually add the milk, whisking until the cornstarch is dissolved. Cook over medium heat, whisking constantly, until the mixture comes to a boil. Place the egg substitute in a small bowl. Whisk in about ½ cup of the hot milk mixture, then whisk the egg mixture back into the saucepan. Return the mixture to a boil, then reduce the heat to medium-low and cook for 1 minute, still whisking. Remove from the heat and whisk in the butter and vanilla.

Serving Size: 1 slice without garnishes
Total Calories: 220
Calories from Fat: 90
Total Fat: 10 g
Saturated Fat: 4.5 g
Cholesterol: 15 mg

Sodium: 200 mg
Total Carbohydrates: 29 g
Dietary Fiber: 1 g
Sugars: 8 g
Protein: 4 g
EXCHANGES PER SERVING
2 starches, 2 fats

5. Arrange the sliced bananas in the bottom of the cooled crust. Pour the filling over the bananas and smooth the top. Place a piece of waxed paper or plastic wrap directly on the surface of the filling to prevent a skin from forming; poke a few holes in the waxed paper to allow steam to escape. Refrigerate until chilled, at least 3 hours or overnight.

6. Remove the waxed paper. Remove the sides of the tart pan. To serve, cut into wedges, garnishing each portion with a dollop of whipped topping and a sprinkle of walnuts, if desired, and serve chilled.

To save time in the kitchen, the recipes in this book were developed with a variety of prepared piecrusts. Refrigerated piecrusts are typically packed with 2 prerolled round piecrusts for 9-inch pies to one 15-ounce package. Frozen pie shells usually come 2 shells to a package, and can be baked frozen, without thawing. Reduced-fat graham cracker crusts can be found in the bakery aisle of the grocery store. If you wish to substitute a homemade piecrust, note that the nutritional information for the recipe will change accordingly.

# pecan pie

This deliciously rich favorite is associated with the South, most probably because of the prevalence of pecan sweets (pralines and the like) below the Mason-Dixon line. It is interesting to note that the first printed recipe for pecan pie didn't appear until well into the twentieth century, so it is hardly an ancient dish. Here's a reduced-sugar recipe for this American dessert icon.

**One 9-inch frozen pie shell**

**3 large eggs**

**¾ cup firmly packed SPLENDA® Brown Sugar Blend**

**¾ cup light corn syrup**

**2 tablespoons unsalted butter, melted**

**1 teaspoon vanilla extract**

**1½ cups pecan halves**

1. Position a rack in the center of the oven and preheat to 350°F. To discourage over-browning, cover the top edges of the pie shell with strips of aluminum foil. Place the pie shell on a baking sheet.

2. Whisk the eggs in a medium bowl until blended. Whisk in the SPLENDA® Brown Sugar Blend, corn syrup, melted butter, and vanilla. Stir in the pecans. Pour into the pastry shell.

3. Bake for 25 minutes. Remove the foil strips. Continue baking until a knife inserted near the center of the pie comes out clean, about 25 minutes more.

4. Transfer the pie to a wire rack and let stand until warm or cooled completely. Cut into wedges and serve.

### NUTRITIONAL INFORMATION

Serving Size: 1 slice
Total Calories: 410
Calories from Fat: 220
Total Fat: 24 g
Saturated Fat: 6 g
Cholesterol: 90 mg

Sodium: 125 mg
Total Carbohydrates: 48 g
Dietary Fiber: 2 g
Sugars: 37 g
Protein: 5 g

**EXCHANGES PER SERVING**
3 starches, 4 fats

# chocolate cream pie

A cool slice of chocolate cream pie brings to mind a well-run country diner with down-to-earth, tasty food that satisfies on many levels. Some of the fat and sugar have been reduced from this version, but its sumptuous profile is intact.

### Filling

**⅔ cup SPLENDA® No Calorie Sweetener, Granulated**

**⅓ cup Dutch-process cocoa powder**

**¼ cup cornstarch**

**⅛ teaspoon salt**

**2½ cups 2% reduced-fat milk**

**½ cup liquid egg substitute**

**1½ tablespoons unsalted butter, at room temperature**

**1 tablespoon vanilla extract**

**One 9-inch reduced-fat graham cracker crust**

**One 8-ounce container reduced-fat frozen whipped topping, thawed**

**Chocolate shavings for garnish (optional)**

1. To make the filling, mix the SPLENDA® Granulated Sweetener, cocoa powder, cornstarch, and salt in a heavy-bottomed medium saucepan. Gradually add the milk, whisking until the cornstarch is dissolved. Cook over medium heat, whisking constantly, until the mixture comes to a boil. Place the egg substitute in a small bowl. Whisk in about ½ cup of the hot milk mixture, then whisk the egg mixture back into the saucepan. Return the mixture to a boil, then reduce the heat to medium-low and cook for 1 minute, still whisking. Remove from the heat and whisk in the butter and vanilla.

2. Pour the filling into the crust and smooth the top. Place a piece of waxed paper or plastic wrap directly on the surface of the filling to prevent a skin from forming; poke a few holes in the waxed paper to allow steam to escape. Refrigerate until chilled, at least 3 hours or overnight.

3. Remove the waxed paper. Spread the whipped topping over the filling. Garnish with the chocolate shavings, if desired. Cut into wedges and serve chilled.

#### NUTRITIONAL INFORMATION

Serving Size: 1 slice without chocolate shavings
Total Calories: 250
Calories from Fat: 100
Total Fat: 11 g
Saturated Fat: 6 g
Cholesterol: 10 mg
Sodium: 230 mg
Total Carbohydrates: 32 g
Dietary Fiber: 1 g
Sugars: 17 g
Protein: 7 g

**EXCHANGES PER SERVING**
2 starches, 2 fats

# mango mojito pie

In the dog days of summer, you just might not care to turn on the oven, even though you might have a hankering for a cool dessert. That's when you should think about this elegant pie. It was inspired by the mojito cocktail, a bracing concoction of rum, crushed mint, and lime juice. For a gorgeous optional topping, arrange mango slices over the top of the filling just before serving.

1 envelope (1 tablespoon) unflavored gelatin

½ cup nonfat milk

One 8-ounce package reduced-fat cream cheese, at room temperature

¾ cup SPLENDA® No Calorie Sweetener, Granulated

1 cup light sour cream, at room temperature

2 tablespoons fresh lime juice

2 teaspoons grated lime zest

½ teaspoon rum extract

2 ripe mangoes, peeled, pitted, cut into ¼-inch dice (see Note)

One 9-inch reduced-fat graham cracker crust

Mint sprigs for garnish

## NUTRITIONAL INFORMATION

Serving Size: 1 slice
Total Calories: 240
Calories from Fat: 90
Total Fat: 10 g
Saturated Fat: 5 g
Cholesterol: 25 mg

Sodium: 260 mg
Total Carbohydrates: 32 g
Dietary Fiber: 1 g
Sugars: 18 g
Protein: 6 g

EXCHANGES PER SERVING
2 starches, 2 fats

1. Sprinkle the gelatin over the milk in a small saucepan. Let stand until the gelatin softens, about 1 minute. Cook over low heat, stirring constantly, until the gelatin dissolves, about 2 minutes.

2. Beat the cream cheese and SPLENDA® Granulated Sweetener in a medium bowl with an electric mixer on high speed until smooth. Gradually beat in the sour cream, lime juice and zest, and rum extract. Gradually beat in the dissolved gelatin mixture. Refrigerate until the filling thickens slightly but is still pourable, about 30 minutes. Fold the mango into the filling.

3. Pour the filling into the crust. Refrigerate again until the filling is set, at least 2 hours or overnight.

4. To serve, cut into wedges and garnish each slice with a mint sprig. Serve chilled.

NOTE: To prepare the mangoes, place one on the work surface. The pit, which is about ½ inch thick, will run horizontally through the center of the fruit. Use a sharp knife to cut off the top of the fruit, coming just above the top of the pit. Repeat to cut off the other side of the fruit. Using a large metal spoon, scoop the mango flesh from each half in one piece. The peeled mango flesh can now be chopped or sliced as required. The pit portion can be pared with a small knife, and the flesh nibbled from the pit as the cook's treat.

# coconut cream pie

Coconut lovers (and even some people who claim that they don't like coconut) will find it impossible to pass up a piece of this timeless masterpiece of American desserts. Use a heavy-bottomed saucepan and whisk constantly when making the filling to avoid scorching. The pie is rich enough without whipped topping, but if you want to give in to temptation, spread a layer on top of the pie before adding the toasted coconut.

1 cup sweetened flaked coconut, divided

*Filling*

¾ cup SPLENDA® No Calorie Sweetener, Granulated

⅓ cup cornstarch

½ teaspoon salt

2½ cups 1% low-fat milk

2 large egg yolks

2 tablespoons unsalted butter

1¼ teaspoons vanilla extract

¼ teaspoon coconut extract

One 9-inch reduced-fat graham cracker crust

### NUTRITIONAL INFORMATION

Serving Size: 1 slice
Total Calories: 290
Calories from Fat: 140
Total Fat: 15 g
Saturated Fat: 7 g
Cholesterol: 60 mg

Sodium: 400 mg
Total Carbohydrates: 35 g
Dietary Fiber: 1 g
Sugars: 19 g
Protein: 5 g

EXCHANGES PER SERVING
2½ starches, 3 fats

1. Position a rack in the center of the oven and preheat to 350°F.

2. Spread ¼ cup of the coconut on a baking sheet. Bake, stirring occasionally, until the coconut is toasted light brown, about 6 minutes. Transfer to a plate and set aside to let cool. Cover loosely with plastic wrap and store at room temperature.

3. To make the filling, mix the SPLENDA® Granulated Sweetener, cornstarch, and salt in a heavy-bottomed medium saucepan. Gradually add the milk, whisking until the cornstarch is dissolved. Cook over medium heat, whisking constantly, until the mixture comes to a boil. Place the egg yolks in a small bowl. Whisk in about ½ cup of the hot milk mixture, then whisk the yolk mixture back into the saucepan. Return the mixture to a boil, then reduce the heat to medium-low and cook for 1 minute, still whisking. Remove from the heat and whisk in the butter and vanilla and coconut extracts, then the remaining coconut.

4. Pour the filling into the crust and smooth the top. Place a piece of waxed paper or plastic wrap directly on the surface of the filling to prevent a skin from forming; poke a few holes in the waxed paper to allow steam to escape. Refrigerate until chilled, at least 3 hours or overnight.

5. Remove the waxed paper. Sprinkle the toasted coconut over the pie. Cut into wedges and serve chilled.

# the great pumpkin pumpkin pie

The Great Pumpkin may make its annual appearance at Halloween, but great pumpkin pie is to be found on practically every Thanksgiving dinner table—and this is indeed a great pumpkin pie recipe. It has a special richness and SPLENDA® No Calorie Sweetener reduces the amount of sugar in the filling.

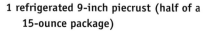

1 refrigerated 9-inch piecrust (half of a 15-ounce package)

3 large eggs

One 15-ounce can solid-pack pumpkin

¾ cup half-and-half

¾ cup SPLENDA® No Calorie Sweetener, Granulated

3 tablespoons SPLENDA® Brown Sugar Blend

1 teaspoon vanilla extract

2 teaspoons ground cinnamon

2 teaspoons ground ginger

⅛ teaspoon ground cloves

½ teaspoon salt

1. Position a rack in the center of the oven and preheat to 375°F.

2. Unroll the piecrust onto a clean work surface. Fit the piecrust into a 9-inch pie pan. Fold the edges of the piecrust under and crimp the edges. Place the pie pan on a baking sheet.

3. Whisk the eggs in a medium bowl. Add the pumpkin, half-and-half, SPLENDA® Granulated Sweetener, SPLENDA® Brown Sugar Blend, vanilla, cinnamon, ginger, cloves, and salt. Whisk just until blended. Pour into the piecrust.

4. Bake until the edges of the crust are golden and a knife inserted near the center of the filling comes out clean, 50 to 60 minutes.

5. Let cool completely on a wire rack. If desired, cover and refrigerate until chilled. To serve, cut into wedges.

### NUTRITIONAL INFORMATION

Serving Size: 1 slice
Total Calories: 230
Calories from Fat: 110
Total Fat: 12 g
Saturated Fat: 3.5 g
Cholesterol: 90 mg

Sodium: 340 mg
Total Carbohydrates: 24 g
Dietary Fiber: 3 g
Sugars: 6 g
Protein: 5 g

**EXCHANGES PER SERVING**
1½ starches, 2 fats

# lemon chiffon pie

This light-as-a-feather chiffon pie will play a trick on your palate. It is so delectable that you'll never guess that it is made with whipped evaporated milk instead of the usual heavy cream. And SPLENDA® No Calorie Sweetener brings the sugar and calories down, as well.

**1 cup evaporated milk**

**1 envelope (1 tablespoon) unflavored gelatin**

**½ cup water**

**¾ cup SPLENDA® No Calorie Sweetener, Granulated**

**3 tablespoons fresh lemon juice**

**¾ teaspoon fresh lemon zest**

**¼ teaspoon lemon extract (optional)**

**One 9-inch reduced-fat graham cracker crust**

**Curls of lemon zest for garnish (optional)**

### NUTRITIONAL INFORMATION

Serving Size: 1 slice
Total Calories: 200
Calories from Fat: 80
Total Fat: 9 g
Saturated Fat: 3 g
Cholesterol: 10 mg

Sodium: 200 mg
Total Carbohydrates: 25 g
Dietary Fiber: 0 g
Sugars: 15 g
Protein: 4 g

EXCHANGES PER SERVING
1½ starches, 2 fats

1. Freeze the evaporated milk in a medium stainless steel mixing bowl until ice crystals begin to form around the edges, about 30 minutes.

2. Meanwhile, sprinkle the gelatin over the water in a small saucepan and let stand for 1 minute to soften the gelatin (see page 182). Stir in the SPLENDA® Granulated Sweetener and heat over low heat, stirring constantly, until the gelatin dissolves, about 2 minutes. Stir in the lemon juice and zest and the extract, if using. Set aside and let cool to room temperature.

3. Whip the icy evaporated milk with an electric mixer on high speed until the milk forms soft peaks, 3 to 5 minutes. Stir one-third of the whipped evaporated milk into the lemon mixture to lighten its texture. Now pour this mixture over the remaining whipped milk and fold them together. Pour into the crust. Place a piece of waxed paper or plastic wrap directly on the surface of the filling to prevent a skin from forming. Refrigerate until the filling is chilled and set, at least 2 hours or overnight.

4. Cut into wedges and serve chilled, garnishing each portion with a curl of lemon zest, if desired.

Gelatin is used to thicken some of these pie fillings. Sprinkle the gelatin evenly over the required liquid, or else it may lump. Cook over very low heat, stirring constantly (a heatproof silicone spatula works best, as it can also scrape down undissolved particles from the sides of the pan) until the gelatin is completely dissolved.

# lofty lemon meringue pie

Are you the kind of dessert lover who savors the top of the lemon meringue pie first? This version takes advantage of easy-to-use dried egg whites to make a topping that rises to dramatic heights.

1 refrigerated 9-inch piecrust
(half of a 15-ounce package)

*Filling*

1¾ cups water

1½ cups SPLENDA® No Calorie Sweetener, Granulated

¼ cup cornstarch

4 egg yolks, lightly beaten

½ cup fresh lemon juice

2 teaspoons grated lemon zest

2 tablespoons unsalted butter

*Meringue*

¾ cup water

¼ cup meringue powder (see Note, page 175)

1 tablespoon cornstarch

½ teaspoon vanilla extract

½ cup SPLENDA® No Calorie Sweetener, Granulated

¼ cup light corn syrup

**NUTRITIONAL INFORMATION**

Serving Size: 1 slice
Total Calories: 250
Calories from Fat: 110
Total Fat: 12 g
Saturated Fat: 6 g
Cholesterol: 115 mg

Sodium: 135 mg
Total Carbohydrates: 33 g
Dietary Fiber: 0 g
Sugars: 10 g
Protein: 2 g

**EXCHANGES PER SERVING**
2 starches, 2 fats

1. Position a rack in the center of the oven and preheat to 450°F.

2. Unroll the piecrust onto a clean work surface. Fit the piecrust into a 9-inch pie pan. Fold the edges of the piecrust under and crimp the edges. Prick the bottom and sides of the piecrust with a fork. Place the piecrust on a baking sheet.

3. Bake until lightly browned, 9 to 11 minutes. Let cool on a wire rack. Reduce the oven temperature to 350°F.

4. To make the filling, whisk the water, SPLENDA® Granulated Sweetener, cornstarch, and egg yolks together in a heavy-bottomed medium saucepan. Cook over medium heat, whisking constantly, until the mixture comes to a boil. Reduce the heat to medium-low and boil, still whisking, for 1 minute. Remove from the heat. Whisk in the lemon juice and zest and the butter. Immediately spread the filling in the cooled piecrust. Set aside.

5. To make the meringue, beat the water, meringue powder, cornstarch, and vanilla in a large, greasefree bowl with an electric mixer on high speed until soft peaks form. Beat in the SPLENDA® Granulated Sweetener, 1 table-spoon at a time, then add the corn syrup and beat until stiff, shiny peaks form. Immediately spread the meringue over the top of the hot filling, being sure that the meringue touches the edges of the piecrust.

6. Bake until the meringue is lightly browned, about 15 minutes. Let cool completely on a wire rack. Cut into wedges and serve.

# red, white, and blueberry tart

This patriotically-hued dessert extravaganza would stop the show at a Fourth of July picnic, but the creamy filling works equally well as a base for other fruits, such as raspberries, peaches, or nectarines, so use your imagination and experiment.

**1 refrigerated 9-inch piecrust (half of a 15-ounce package)**

*Filling*

**½ cup SPLENDA® No Calorie Sweetener, Granulated**

**2 tablespoons cornstarch**

**Pinch of salt**

**1 cup 2% reduced-fat milk**

**2 large eggs**

**4 ounces reduced-fat cream cheese, at room temperature**

**1 teaspoon vanilla extract**

1. Position a rack in the center of the oven and preheat to 450°F.

2. Unroll the piecrust onto a clean work surface. Fit the piecrust into a 9-inch round tart pan with a removable bottom, being sure that the dough fits tightly where the bottom of the pan meets the sides. Trim the piecrust edges level with the top of the pan. Line the piecrust with aluminum foil, then fill with pie weights or dried beans. Place the pie pan on a baking sheet.

3. Bake until the edges of the crust begin to brown, about 8 minutes. Lift off the foil and weights and continue baking until the crust is lightly browned, 5 to 7 minutes. Let cool completely on a wire rack.

4. To make the filling, mix the SPLENDA® Granulated Sweetener, cornstarch, and salt together in a heavy-bottomed medium saucepan. Gradually add the milk and whisk until the cornstarch is dissolved. Cook over medium heat, whisking constantly, until the mixture comes to a boil. Lightly beat the eggs in a small bowl. Whisk about half of the milk mixture into the eggs, then whisk the egg mixture back into the saucepan. Return to a boil and cook, whisking constantly, for 1 minute. Remove from heat.

5. Beat the cream cheese in a medium bowl with an electric mixer on high speed until smooth. Gradually beat in the hot milk mixture until smooth and blended. Beat in the vanilla. Spread evenly in the cooled piecrust. Place a piece of waxed paper or plastic wrap directly on the surface of the filling to prevent a skin from forming; poke a few holes in the waxed paper to allow steam to escape. Refrigerate until the filling is cool, about 2 hours.

## Topping

1 pint fresh blueberries

1 pint fresh strawberries, hulled

1 teaspoon unflavored gelatin

½ cup water

1½ tablespoons SPLENDA® No Calorie Sweetener, Granulated

1½ tablespoons fresh lemon juice

6. To prepare the topping, arrange the blueberries and strawberries in a pattern on top of the filling. Sprinkle the gelatin over the water in a small saucepan. Let stand for 1 minute to soften the gelatin (see page 182). Stir in the SPLENDA® Granulated Sweetener and the lemon juice. Heat over very low heat, stirring constantly, until the gelatin dissolves, about 2 minutes. Spoon the gelatin mixture evenly over the berries until the berries are coated; discard any remaining gelatin mixture. Refrigerate until the filling is chilled and the topping sets, about 1 hour.

7. To serve, remove the sides of the tart pan. Cut into wedges and serve chilled.

Cooked pie fillings need to be cooked for a full minute after they come to their original boil. This ensures a firm set. If the filling is undercooked, the filling could separate when chilled. Also, whisk the filling constantly throughout the cooking period, and keep an eye on the heat level during the final 1-minute boil to avoid scorching.

# cranberry-walnut tartlets

It's hard to believe, but armed with a mini-muffin pan, a cookie cutter, and refrigerated piecrust, you can have 2 dozen beautiful tartlets ready for the oven in a surprisingly short amount of time. These bite-sized beauties, glistening with fresh red cranberries, will be the star of a winter buffet, or tuck them amongst your annual selection of holiday cookies. Toasting the nuts will give the tartlets a deeper, nuttier flavor, but you can skip this step if you're in a hurry.

¼ cup (1 ounce) walnut pieces

1 refrigerated 9-inch piecrust (half of a 15-ounce package)

Flour for rolling the piecrust

½ cup SPLENDA® No Calorie Sweetener, Granulated

1 large egg, lightly beaten

3 tablespoons light corn syrup

1 cup chopped fresh cranberries

### NUTRITIONAL INFORMATION

Serving Size: 1 tartlet  
Total Calories: 60  
Calories from Fat: 30  
Total Fat: 3.5 g  
Saturated Fat: 1 g  
Cholesterol: 10 mg  

Sodium: 40 mg  
Total Carbohydrates: 8 g  
Dietary Fiber: 0 g  
Sugars: 3 g  
Protein: 1 g  

EXCHANGES PER SERVING  
½ starch, 1 fat

1. Position a rack in the center of the oven and preheat to 350°F. Have ready a standard 24-cup mini-muffin pan.

2. If desired, spread the walnuts on a baking sheet and bake, stirring occasionally, until toasted, about 10 minutes. Transfer to a plate and let cool.

3. Unroll the piecrust onto a lightly floured work surface and dust the top with flour. Roll the piecrust to ⅛-inch thickness. Using a 2¼-inch round cookie cutter, cut the piecrust into 24 rounds. Fit each round into a muffin cup. Place the muffin pan in the freezer for 10 minutes.

4. Meanwhile, chop the walnuts. Whisk the SPLENDA® Granulated Sweetener and egg in a medium bowl. Whisk in the corn syrup. Stir in the cranberries and chopped walnuts. Spoon equal amounts of the cranberry mixture into each tartlet shell.

5. Bake until the edges of the pastry are golden and the filling is set, 15 to 20 minutes. Let cool in the pan on a wire rack for 10 minutes. If needed, carefully run the tip of a dull knife between the shell and pan to release the tartlets, then remove the tartlets from the pan. Let cool completely on the rack, then serve.

# strawberry rhubarb pie

A juicy strawberry and rhubarb pie is a harbinger of late spring. While rhubarb may not seem a promising ingredient on its own, paired with strawberries, it becomes extraordinary. Look for young, pale stalks, as these are the least fibrous. If the strawberries are properly red and ripe, the filling will be properly red, but if you have any doubts, add a drop or two of red food coloring (don't overdo it!).

**¾ cup SPLENDA® No Calorie Sweetener, Granulated**

**3 tablespoons cornstarch**

**3½ cups sliced rhubarb**

**2½ cups sliced strawberries**

**2 refrigerated 9-inch piecrusts (one 15-ounce package)**

**Flour for rolling out piecrust**

---

NUTRITIONAL INFORMATION

| | |
|---|---|
| Serving Size: 1 slice | Total Carbohydrates: 37 g |
| Total Calories: 290 | Dietary Fiber: 2 g |
| Calories from Fat: 130 | Sugars: 6 g |
| Total Fat: 14 g | Protein: 3 g |
| Saturated Fat: 6 g | **EXCHANGES PER SERVING** |
| Cholesterol: 10 mg | 1½ starches, 1 fruit, |
| Sodium: 200 mg | 3 fats |

1. Position a rack in the center of the oven and preheat to 375°F.

2. Mix the SPLENDA® Granulated Sweetener and cornstarch in a medium bowl. Add the rhubarb and strawberries and mix gently.

3. Unroll 1 piecrust onto a clean work surface. Line a 9-inch pie pan with the piecrust. Trim the piecrust edges to extend ½ inch beyond the edge of the pan. Pour the fruit mixture into the pie shell. Unroll the second piecrust onto a lightly floured work surface and lightly flour the top. Using a rolling pin, roll out the dough into ⅛-inch thickness. Place the dough over the filling. Fold the edges of the top dough under the bottom crust and crimp the edges. Cut slits in the top dough to allow steam to escape. Place the pie on a baking sheet.

4. Bake until the juices are bubbling out of the slits and the crust is golden, 40 to 50 minutes. If the crust seems to be browning too quickly, tent it with aluminum foil. Let cool completely on a wire rack. Cut into wedges and serve.

cookies

# almond-raisin biscotti

Double-baking gives biscotti their delightful crispness. Dunked into a cup of coffee or tea, they transform instantly into tender mouthfuls. This version is also excellent with dried cherries standing in for the raisins. A chocolate variation follows the main recipe (see page 98).

**Nonstick cooking spray for the baking sheet**

**2 cups all-purpose flour**

**1 teaspoon baking powder**

**1 teaspoon baking soda**

**⅛ teaspoon salt**

**1½ cups SPLENDA® No Calorie Sweetener, Granulated**

**3 large eggs, at room temperature, plus 1 large egg, lightly beaten for glazing**

**2 tablespoons whole milk**

**¼ teaspoon almond extract**

**1 cup slivered almonds, toasted (see Note)**

**½ cup raisins**

1. Position a rack in the center of the oven and preheat to 350°F. Lightly spray a baking sheet with the cooking spray.

2. Sift together the flour, baking powder, baking soda, and salt into a bowl. Beat the SPLENDA® Granulated Sweetener, the 3 eggs, and milk in a large bowl with an electric mixer at high speed until the mixture is thick and pale yellow, about 3 minutes. Beat in the almond extract. Reduce the speed to low, add the flour mixture, and mix until combined. (If you aren't using a heavy-duty mixer, you may have to stir in the flour mixture.) Stir in the almonds and raisins.

3. Turn out the dough onto a lightly floured work surface. Knead 4 or 5 times to smooth out the dough. Divide the dough in half. Form each portion into an 8-inch-long log. Place the logs, at least 2 inches apart, on the prepared baking sheet. Flatten each log to ¾-inch thickness. Lightly brush the tops of the logs with the beaten egg.

4. Bake until the logs are puffed and golden brown, about 20 minutes. Leaving the oven on, transfer the logs from the baking sheet to a wire rack and let cool for 10 minutes. Using a gentle sawing motion, cut each log diagonally into 16 slices about ½ inch thick with a serrated knife.

**NOTE:** To toast almonds (and pecans), spread the nuts on a rimmed baking sheet. Bake in a preheated 350°F oven, stirring occasionally, until fragrant and toasted, about 10 minutes. Cool completely.

> CONTINUED

Serving Size: 1 cookie
Total Calories: 70
Calories from Fat: 20
Total Fat: 2 g
Saturated Fat: 0 g
Cholesterol: 25 mg

Sodium: 70 mg
Total Carbohydrates: 10 g
Dietary Fiber: 1 g
Sugars: 2 g
Protein: 2 g
**EXCHANGES PER SERVING**
½ starch, 1 fat

**VARIATION
CHOCOLATE-ALMOND BISCOTTI**

Serving Size: 1 cookie
Total Calories: 60
Calories from Fat: 25
Total Fat: 2.5 g
Saturated Fat: 0 g
Cholesterol: 25 mg

Sodium: 70 mg
Total Carbohydrates: 8 g
Dietary Fiber: 1 g
Sugars: 0 g
Protein: 2 g
**EXCHANGES PER SERVING**
½ starch, 1 fat

**5.** Return the slices, cut side down, to the baking sheet. Bake for 10 minutes. Turn the slices over and bake until the biscotti are crisp, about 10 minutes more. Let cool briefly on the baking sheets, then transfer to wire racks and let cool completely. Store the cookies at room temperature in an airtight container.

*Variation*

**CHOCOLATE-ALMOND BISCOTTI:** Omit the raisins. Substitute 1¾ cups all-purpose flour and ⅓ cup unsweetened non-alkalized cocoa powder for the 2 cups all-purpose flour.

Instead of greasing baking sheets, consider lining the sheets with parchment (baking) paper or silicone baking pads. These products let you use the sheets a couple of times before washing, which is handy when baking large batches of cookies for holidays. Be sure to let the baking sheets cool between uses or the cookie dough will begin to melt before it goes into the oven, making misshapen cookies.

# coffee toffee bars

Three layers—a crisp bottom crust, a chewy toffee filling, and a final topping of chocolate and pecans—make these cookies special. They are rich and perfect for nibbling with a cup of strong espresso. You'll need a candy thermometer for making the toffee layer.

### Crust

**Nonstick cooking spray for the pan**

**½ cup firmly packed SPLENDA®
Brown Sugar Blend**

**4 tablespoons unsalted butter,
at room temperature**

**1 large egg yolk**

**1 cup all-purpose flour**

**¼ teaspoon salt**

### Toffee Layer

**1 cup firmly packed SPLENDA®
Brown Sugar Blend**

**½ cup light corn syrup**

**½ cup evaporated milk**

**4 tablespoons unsalted butter,
at room temperature**

**1½ teaspoons vanilla extract**

> CONTINUED

1. Position a rack in the center of the oven and preheat to 350°F. Lightly spray a 9-by-13-inch baking pan with the cooking spray.

2. To make the crust, beat the SPLENDA® Brown Sugar Blend and butter in a medium bowl with an electric mixer on medium speed until blended, about 1 minute. Add the egg yolk and beat until combined. Reduce the speed to low, add the flour and salt, and beat just until the mixture forms fine crumbs. Press the dough evenly into the bottom of the prepared pan.

3. Bake the crust until golden, 12 to 15 minutes. Transfer to a wire rack. Keep the oven on.

4. To make the toffee layer, combine the SPLENDA® Brown Sugar Blend, corn syrup, evaporated milk, and butter in a medium, heavy-bottomed saucepan. Attach a candy thermometer to the saucepan. Cook over low heat, stirring constantly, until the SPLENDA® dissolves. Raise the heat to medium. Cook, stirring occasionally with a wooden spoon to prevent scorching, until the toffee reaches 265°F, about 10 minutes. Stir in the vanilla. Spread the toffee evenly over the crust. Bake until bubbling throughout, about 10 minutes. Let cool on a wire rack for 5 minutes.

> CONTINUED

### Chocolate-Pecan Topping

**3 ounces unsweetened chocolate, finely chopped**

**2 tablespoons SPLENDA®
Brown Sugar Blend**

**1 cup pecans, toasted (see Note, page 96) and chopped**

NUTRITIONAL INFORMATION

Serving Size: 1 cookie
Total Calories: 150
Calories from Fat: 70
Total Fat: 8 g
Saturated Fat: 3 g
Cholesterol: 15 mg

Sodium: 30 mg
Total Carbohydrates: 20 g
Dietary Fiber: 1 g
Sugars: 15 g
Protein: 2 g

EXCHANGES PER SERVING
1½ starches, 1 fat

5. Meanwhile, make the chocolate-pecan topping: Combine the chocolate and SPLENDA® Brown Sugar Blend in the top of a double boiler or a heatproof bowl nested on top of a saucepan over (but not touching) simmering water and heat, stirring occasionally, until the chocolate melts. Remove from the heat. Spread the melted chocolate over the toffee layer and sprinkle with the pecans.

6. Let cool completely on the wire rack. If necessary, refrigerate to chill and set the chocolate layer, about 10 minutes. Cut into 30 bars or diamond-shaped pieces. Store the bars in an airtight container.

# gingerbread cookies

Everyone needs a great gingerbread cookie recipe for making holiday cutout cookies. Depending on the size of the cookie cutter, this will make at least 4 dozen spicy treats. Refrigerate the dough for at least 2 hours before rolling out, which makes the dough easier to handle and allows the spices to mingle.

**6 cups all-purpose flour**

**1 tablespoon plus 1 teaspoon ground ginger**

**1 tablespoon plus 1 teaspoon ground cinnamon**

**1½ teaspoons ground cloves**

**1 teaspoon salt**

**1 teaspoon baking soda**

**½ teaspoon baking powder**

**1 cup (2 sticks) unsalted butter, at room temperature**

**1 cup SPLENDA® No Calorie Sweetener, Granulated**

**2 large eggs, at room temperature**

**1 cup unsulfured molasses**

**3 tablespoons water**

1. Sift together the flour, ginger, cinnamon, cloves, salt, baking soda, and baking powder into a bowl.

2. Beat the butter and SPLENDA® Granulated Sweetener in a large bowl with an electric mixer on high speed until combined, about 1 minute. One at a time, beat in the eggs, mixing well after each addition. Beat in the molasses and water. Gradually stir in the flour mixture to make a stiff dough. Divide the dough in half and put each portion in a zippered plastic bag. Refrigerate until well chilled, at least 2 hours or overnight.

3. Position racks in the center and upper third of the oven and preheat to 350°F.

4. If the chilled dough is too hard to roll out, let stand at room temperature for a few minutes, just until pliable. Working with one portion of dough at a time, unwrap the dough and place on a lightly floured work surface. Lightly flour the top of the dough and roll out the dough to slightly less than ¼ inch thick. Cut into desired shapes with cookie cutters. Place the cookies, 1 inch apart, on ungreased baking sheets.

5. Bake the cookies until lightly browned on the bottoms (lift one gently with a spatula to check), 8 to 10 minutes.

6. Let cool briefly on the baking sheets, then transfer the cookies to wire racks and let cool completely. Decorate as desired. Store the cookies at room temperature in an airtight container.

### NUTRITIONAL INFORMATION

Serving Size: One 2-inch cookie

Total Calories: 100

Calories from Fat: 35

Total Fat: 3.5 g

Saturated Fat: 2 g

Cholesterol: 15 mg

Sodium: 75 mg

Total Carbohydrates: 16 g

Dietary Fiber: 0 g

Sugars: 4 g

Protein: 2 g

**EXCHANGES PER SERVING**

1 starch, 1 fat

# chocolate chip cookies

If ever there was an all-American cookie, the chocolate chip cookie is it. If you have any leftovers, wrap each cookie in plastic wrap, slide into zippered freezer bags, and freeze until you have your next craving.

2¼ cups all-purpose flour

1 teaspoon baking soda

1 teaspoon salt

1 cup (2 sticks) unsalted butter, at room temperature

¼ cup SPLENDA® Sugar Blend

¼ cup firmly packed SPLENDA® Brown Sugar Blend

1 teaspoon vanilla extract

2 large eggs, at room temperature

One 12-ounce package Nestle Toll House semisweet chocolate morsels

**NUTRITIONAL INFORMATION**

Serving Size: 1 cookie
Total Calories: 90
Calories from Fat: 50
Total Fat: 5 g
Saturated Fat: 3.5 g
Cholesterol: 15 g
Sodium: 70 g
Total Carbohydrates: 11 g
Dietary Fiber: 1 g
Sugars: 6 g
Protein: 1 g

**EXCHANGES PER SERVING**
½ starch, 1 fat

1. Position racks in the center and upper third of the oven and preheat to 375°F.

2. Sift together the flour, baking soda, and salt into a bowl. Beat the butter, SPLENDA® Sugar Blend, SPLENDA® Brown Sugar Blend, and vanilla in a large bowl with an electric mixer on medium speed until blended, about 2 minutes. One at a time, beat in the eggs, mixing well after each addition. On low speed, gradually beat in the flour mixture. Stir in the chocolate morsels. Drop rounded tablespoons of the dough, 1 inch apart, onto ungreased baking sheets.

3. Bake until the cookies are lightly browned, 9 to 11 minutes.

4. Let cool briefly on the baking sheets, then transfer the cookies to wire racks and let cool completely. Store the cookies at room temperature in an airtight container.

For the best results, bake cookies on large, heavy aluminum baking sheets. Flimsy cookie sheets lead to burned cookie bottoms. Professional bakers swear by the 17-by-12-inch baking sheets called "half-sheet" pans. They hold a lot of cookies and the heavy-gauge metal doesn't warp easily.

# spritz cookies

While these beautifully shaped, charming cookies are a must for the December holiday cookie display, they are also perfect for tea time. You will need a cookie press, available at kitchenware stores. By changing the plate insert, you can create many different shapes. For a bit of color, place chopped dried cherries or apricots in the center of each cookie, if you wish.

**Nonstick cooking spray for the baking sheets**

**2 cups all-purpose flour, plus more if needed**

**½ teaspoon baking powder**

**1 cup (2 sticks) unsalted butter, at room temperature**

**1 cup SPLENDA® No Calorie Sweetener, Granulated**

**2 teaspoons vanilla extract**

**¼ teaspoon almond extract**

**1 large egg yolk, plus 1 large egg**

### NUTRITIONAL INFORMATION

Serving Size: 2 cookies
Total Calories: 130
Calories from Fat: 80
Total Fat: 9 g
Saturated Fat: 5 g
Cholesterol: 40 mg

Sodium: 100 mg
Total Carbohydrates: 10 g
Dietary Fiber: 0 g
Sugars: 0 g
Protein: 2 g

**EXCHANGES PER SERVING**
½ starch, 2 fats

1. Position racks in the center and upper third of the oven and preheat to 350°F. Lightly spray the baking sheets with the cooking spray.

2. Sift together the flour and baking powder into a bowl. Beat the butter, SPLENDA® Granulated Sweetener, and vanilla and almond extracts in a large bowl with an electric mixer on high speed until well combined, about 2 minutes. Beat in the egg yolk, mixing well, then the whole egg. On low speed, gradually beat in the flour mixture, mixing just until blended.

3. Fit a cookie press with the desired plate and fill the press cylinder with some of the dough. (If the dough is too soft and doesn't hold its shape, return the dough to the bowl and mix in an additional 2 tablespoons of flour thoroughly.) Press the cookies, 1 inch apart, onto the prepared baking sheets.

4. Bake until the cookies are lightly browned on the bottoms (lift one gently with a spatula to check), 10 to 12 minutes.

5. Let cool on the baking sheets for 5 minutes, then transfer to wire racks and let cool completely. Store the cookies at room temperature in an airtight container.

# oatmeal-raisin cookies

These crisp-but-chewy old-fashioned treats are full of flavor. Served with a tall glass of cold milk, they can brighten any dreary afternoon. For the most delectable texture, use old-fashioned rolled oats, instead of quick-cooking or instant.

**Nonstick cooking spray for the baking sheets**

**1½ cups all-purpose flour**

**1 teaspoon baking soda**

**1 teaspoon ground cinnamon**

**1 cup (2 sticks) unsalted butter, at room temperature**

**1 cup SPLENDA® Sugar Blend**

**2 large eggs, at room temperature**

**1 tablespoon unsulfured molasses**

**1½ teaspoons vanilla extract**

**3 cups old-fashioned rolled oats**

**1 cup raisins**

1. Position racks in the center and upper third of the oven and preheat to 350°F. Lightly spray 2 baking sheets with the cooking spray.

2. Sift together the flour, baking soda, and cinnamon into a bowl. Beat the butter and SPLENDA® Sugar Blend in a large bowl with an electric mixer on high speed until light and fluffy, about 3 minutes. One at a time, beat in the eggs, mixing well after each addition. Beat in the molasses and vanilla. On low speed, gradually beat in the flour mixture. Stir in the oats and raisins. Drop rounded tablespoons of the dough, 1 inch apart, onto the prepared baking sheets.

3. Bake until the cookies are lightly browned, 10 to 12 minutes.

4. Let cool briefly on the baking sheets, then transfer the cookies to wire racks and let cool completely. Store the cookies at room temperature in an airtight container.

If you use small cookie sheets, the cookies will have to be baked on two oven racks. For even baking and browning, halfway through baking, switch the position of the sheets from top to bottom and turn them from front to back.

### NUTRITIONAL INFORMATION

Serving Size: 1 cookie
Total Calories: 130
Calories from Fat: 50
Total Fat: 6 g
Saturated Fat: 3.5 g
Cholesterol: 25 mg

Sodium: 90 mg
Total Carbohydrates: 18 g
Dietary Fiber: 0 g
Sugars: 8 g
Protein: 2 g

**EXCHANGES PER SERVING**
1 starch, 1 fat

# sugar cookies

Here's a reduced-sugar version of the classic cutout cookie. The dough is buttery and sweet, and perfect for stamping out shapes with cookie cutters that bake up tender and crisp.

**Nonstick cooking spray for the baking sheets**

**4 cups all-purpose flour, plus more for dusting**

**1 teaspoon baking powder**

**½ teaspoon salt**

**1 cup (2 sticks) unsalted butter, at room temperature**

**1 cup SPLENDA® Sugar Blend**

**2 large eggs, at room temperature**

**2 teaspoons vanilla extract**

### NUTRITIONAL INFORMATION

Serving Size: 1 cookie
Total Calories: 150
Calories from Fat: 60
Total Fat: 7 g
Saturated Fat: 4 g
Cholesterol: 30 mg

Sodium: 60 mg
Total Carbohydrates: 19 g
Dietary Fiber: 0 g
Sugars: 7 g
Protein: 2 g

EXCHANGES PER SERVING
1½ starches, 1 fat

1. Position racks in the center and upper third of the oven and preheat to 325°F. Lightly spray 2 baking sheets with the cooking spray.

2. Sift together the flour, baking powder, and salt into a bowl. Beat the butter in a large bowl with an electric mixer on high speed until creamy, about 1 minute. Gradually beat in the SPLENDA® Sugar Blend until well mixed, about 2 minutes. One at a time, beat in the eggs, mixing well after each addition. Beat in the vanilla. On low speed, gradually beat in the flour mixture, mixing just until blended.

3. Divide the dough in half. Form each portion into a thick disk and wrap in plastic wrap. Refrigerate until well chilled and firm enough to roll out, about 1 hour or until slightly firm.

4. If the chilled dough is too hard to roll out, let stand at room temperature for a few minutes, just until pliable. Working with one portion of dough at a time, unwrap the dough and place on a lightly floured work surface. Lightly flour the top of the dough and roll out to ⅛ inch thickness. Cut into desired shapes with cookie cutters. Place the cookies, 1 inch apart, on the prepared baking sheets.

5. Bake until the cookies are lightly browned, 8 to 10 minutes.

6. Let the cookies cool on the baking sheets for 5 minutes, then transfer to wire racks and let cool completely. Store the cookies at room temperature in an airtight container.

# scrumptious chocolate-coconut squares

Rich and dense, these delectable bars are perfect for making with kids since the recipe requires only the most basic baking skills—and grownups will like the bars because of the very easy cleanup. By making use of modern reduced-fat and reduced-sugar ingredients, these bars are significantly lower in calories than old-fashioned recipes.

½ cup (1 stick) unsalted butter,
    thinly sliced

1½ cups graham cracker crumbs
    (see page 127)

1 cup chopped walnuts

1 cup sweetened flaked coconut, divided

1½ cups Nestle Toll House milk
    chocolate morsels

1 cup low-fat Carnation evaporated milk

½ cup SPLENDA® Sugar Blend

### NUTRITIONAL INFORMATION

Serving Size: 1 bar
Total Calories: 90
Calories from Fat: 50
Total Fat: 5 g
Saturated Fat: 2.5 g
Cholesterol: 5 mg

Sodium: 35 mg
Total Carbohydrates: 10 g
Dietary Fiber: 1 g
Sugars: 8 g
Protein: 2 g

**EXCHANGES PER SERVING**
½ starch, 1 fat

1. Position a rack in the center of the oven and preheat to 350°F.

2. Scatter the butter in a 9-by-13-inch baking pan. Place in the oven and bake to melt the butter, about 2 minutes. Remove the pan from the oven. Tilt the melted butter in the pan to coat ½ inch up the sides. Add the graham cracker crumbs to the pan and stir to moisten the crumbs. Press the crumbs evenly in the bottom of the pan.

3. In the following order, sprinkle the graham cracker–crumb layer with the walnuts, ½ cup of the coconut, and the chocolate morsels. Mix the evaporated milk and SPLENDA® Sugar Blend in a small bowl; pour evenly over the top and spread smooth with a rubber spatula. Sprinkle with the remaining ½ cup coconut.

4. Bake until the top is light golden brown, 25 to 30 minutes.

5. Let cool completely in the pan on a wire rack, about 4 hours. Refrigerate until the filling is set, about 1 hour more. Cut into 48 bars. Store the bars at room temperature in an airtight container.

cheesecakes

# classic cheesecake

What makes a cheesecake "classic"? By many estimates, a cookie-crumb crust covered with a filling full of the distinctive, tangy flavor of cream cheese, accented with lemon zest and vanilla. One bite of this reduced-calorie version and you'll be transported to New York, where cheesecake is king.

### Crust

Nonstick cooking spray for the pan

1¼ cups graham cracker crumbs (see page 127)

4 tablespoons unsalted butter, melted

### Filling

Three 8-ounce packages cream cheese, softened (see page 117)

1 cup SPLENDA® No Calorie Sweetener, Granulated

¼ cup whole milk

2 tablespoons all-purpose flour

2 teaspoons vanilla extract

2 teaspoons grated lemon zest

3 large eggs, at room temperature

#### NUTRITIONAL INFORMATION

Serving Size: 1 slice
Total Calories: 230
Calories from Fat: 170
Total Fat: 19 g
Saturated Fat: 12 g
Cholesterol: 95 mg

Sodium: 210 mg
Total Carbohydrates: 9 g
Dietary Fiber: 0 g
Sugars: 2 g
Protein: 5 g

**EXCHANGES PER SERVING**
½ starch, 4 fats

1. Position a rack in the center of the oven and preheat to 350°F. Lightly spray the inside of a 9-inch springform pan with the cooking spray.

2. To make the crust, mix the graham cracker crumbs and melted butter in a medium bowl until the crumbs are evenly moistened. Press the crumb mixture evenly into the bottom and ½ inch up the sides of the prepared pan.

3. Bake until the crust is lightly browned, about 10 minutes. Let cool on a wire rack while making the filling. Reduce the oven temperature to 325°F.

4. To make the filling, beat the cream cheese in a large bowl with an electric mixer on medium speed until creamy, about 1 minute. Gradually beat in the SPLENDA® Granulated Sweetener, then the milk, and then the flour, vanilla, and lemon zest, scraping down the sides of the bowl often, just until the mixture is smooth. One at a time, beat in the eggs, mixing just until each one is incorporated. Pour into the cooled crust and smooth the top.

5. Bake until the sides of the filling are slightly puffed and the center is almost set, 50 to 60 minutes.

6. Transfer to a wire rack and run a knife around the inside of the pan to release the cheesecake. Let cool completely. Cover with plastic wrap and refrigerate until well chilled, at least 8 hours or overnight.

7. To serve, remove the sides of the pan. Cut into wedges with a sharp, wet knife and serve chilled.

# pumpkin cheesecake

The next time you are asked to bring a dish to a Thanksgiving potluck, think of this rich, creamy, alternative to pumpkin pie. It feeds a crowd, can be made well ahead of time, and is easy to transport. And everyone is sure to enjoy this lightened-up but still luxuriously holiday-spirited dessert.

### Crust

**Nonstick cooking spray for the pan**

**1 cup graham cracker crumbs**
   **(see page 127)**

**¼ cup SPLENDA® No Calorie Sweetener,**
   **Granulated**

**1½ teaspoons ground cinnamon**

**5 tablespoons light butter, melted**

### Filling

**Three 8-ounce packages nonfat cream**
   **cheese, at room temperature**

**Two 8-ounce packages reduced-fat**
   **cream cheese, at room temperature**

**1½ cups SPLENDA® No Calorie Sweetener,**
   **Granulated**

**3 tablespoons all-purpose flour**

**2 teaspoons ground cinnamon**

**¾ teaspoon ground ginger**

**½ teaspoon ground nutmeg**

**Pinch of ground cloves**

**One 15-ounce can solid-pack pumpkin**

**½ cup liquid egg substitute**

**¼ cup fat-free half-and-half**

**1 tablespoon vanilla extract**

1. Position a rack in the center of the oven and preheat to 350°F. Lightly spray the inside of a 9-inch springform pan with the cooking spray.

2. To make the crust, mix the crumbs, SPLENDA® Granulated Sweetener, cinnamon, and butter in a medium bowl until the crumbs are evenly moistened. Press the crumb mixture evenly into the bottom of the prepared pan.

3. Bake until the crust is lightly browned, about 10 minutes. Let cool on a wire rack while making the filling.

4. To make the filling, beat the cream cheeses in a large bowl with an electric mixer on medium speed until creamy. Gradually beat in the SPLENDA® Granulated Sweetener, then the flour, cinnamon, ginger, nutmeg, and cloves, scraping the sides of the bowl often, just until the mixture is smooth. Beat in the pumpkin and mix until blended. Scrape the bowl well, and beat in the egg substitute, half-and-half, and vanilla just until they are incorporated. Pour into the cooled crust and smooth the top.

5. Bake until the sides of the filling are slightly puffed and the center is almost set, 50 to 60 minutes.

## Topping

**2 cups reduced-fat sour cream**

**½ cup SPLENDA® No Calorie Sweetener, Granulated**

**1 teaspoon vanilla extract**

**A few drops maple extract (optional)**

NUTRITIONAL INFORMATION

Serving Size: 1 slice

Total Calories: 180

Calories from Fat: 90

Total Fat: 10 g

Saturated Fat: 6 g

Cholesterol: 30 mg

Sodium: 320 mg

Total Carbohydrates: 14 g

Dietary Fiber: 1 g

Sugars: 3 g

Protein: 10 g

EXCHANGES PER SERVING

1 starch, 1 medium fat meat, 1 fat

**6.** Meanwhile, make the topping: Whisk the sour cream, SPLENDA® Granulated Sweetener, vanilla, and maple extract, if using, until blended. Remove the cheesecake from the oven and spread evenly with the topping. Return to the oven and bake until the topping looks set, about 15 minutes.

**7.** Transfer to a wire rack and run a knife around the inside of the pan to release the cheesecake. Let cool completely. Cover with plastic wrap and refrigerate until well chilled, at least 8 hours or overnight.

**8.** To serve, remove the sides of the pan. Cut into wedges with a sharp, wet knife and serve chilled.

Springform pans are indispensable for baking cheesecakes. The smaller 7-inch pans are perfect when relatively few servings are needed, or for gift-sized cakes. Larger cheesecakes are made in the common 9- or 10-inch pans; these big cheesecakes are great for entertaining crowds, especially during holiday time. Springform pans are available in kitchenware stores and online.

Springform pans can lose their tight seal around the bottom insert with time, and may leak out of the pan into your oven if the cake has a buttery crust. Guard against this by wrapping the outside bottom of the pan tightly in aluminum foil.

# no-bake cheesecake with raspberry sauce

Chocolate, vanilla, and raspberry—what a trio of flavors for a special cheesecake! Using reduced-fat dairy ingredients and SPLENDA® No Calorie Sweetener lessens the calories of this traditional recipe by more than half. And a final enticement—you won't have to turn the oven on, making this a great summertime dessert.

### Crust
**Nonstick cooking spray for the pan**

**1¼ cups chocolate wafer crumbs (about 24 cookies)**

**3 tablespoons light margarine, melted**

### Filling
**1 cup nonfat milk**

**1 cup SPLENDA® No Calorie Sweetener, Granulated**

**1 envelope (1 tablespoon) unflavored gelatin**

**Two 8-ounce packages nonfat cream cheese, softened**

**One 8-ounce package reduced-fat cream cheese, softened**

**½ cup plain nonfat yogurt**

**2 teaspoons vanilla extract**

**¼ teaspoon almond extract**

1. Lightly spray the inside of a 7-inch round springform pan with the cooking spray.

2. To make the crust, mix the cookie crumbs and melted margarine in a small bowl until the crumbs are moistened. Press the crumb mixture evenly into the bottom and ½ inch up the sides of the prepared pan.

3. To make the filling, mix the milk and SPLENDA® Granulated Sweetener in a medium saucepan. Sprinkle the gelatin over the milk and let stand for 1 minute to soften the gelatin (see page 182). Heat over medium heat, stirring constantly with a heatproof silicone spatula, until the milk is hot and the gelatin is completely dissolved. Place the saucepan in a bowl of iced water and stir just until the milk mixture is lukewarm.

4. Beat the cream cheeses in a large bowl with an electric mixer on medium speed until creamy, about 2 minutes. Add the yogurt and vanilla and almond extracts and beat until combined, about 30 seconds. Gradually beat in the milk mixture until smooth. Pour into the crust and smooth the top.

5. Cover with plastic wrap and refrigerate until the filling is set and chilled, at least 2 hours.

### Raspberry Sauce

**One 12-ounce package frozen raspberries, thawed**

**3 tablespoons SPLENDA® No Calorie Sweetener, Granulated**

**1 teaspoon cornstarch**

**1 tablespoon water**

NUTRITIONAL INFORMATION

Serving Size: 1 slice
Total Calories: 160
Calories from Fat: 50
Total Fat: 6 g
Saturated Fat: 2.5 g
Cholesterol: 15 mg

Sodium: 340 mg
Total Carbohydrates: 17 g
Dietary Fiber: 1 g
Sugars: 6 g
Protein: 10 g

EXCHANGES PER SERVING
1½ starches, 1 medium fat meat

6. Meanwhile, make the sauce: Purée the raspberries and their juices and the SPLENDA® Granulated Sweetener in a blender or food processor. Rub the purée through a fine-mesh sieve into a small saucepan; discard the seeds. Sprinkle the cornstarch over the water in a custard cup or ramekin and stir with a fork to dissolve. Stir into the saucepan. Bring to a boil over medium heat, stirring often. Remove from the heat and let cool completely.

7. To serve, run a knife around the inside of the pan to release the cheesecake. Remove the sides of the pan. Cut the cheesecake into wedges with a sharp, wet knife. Serve chilled, drizzling raspberry sauce over each serving.

Cream cheese generally comes in three different fat contents: full-fat (regular), reduced-fat, and nonfat. In all cases, the cheese must be thoroughly softened before making the cheesecake batter, a step that requires patience. Unwrap the chilled cream cheese, chop it into chunks, and place in a bowl. Let stand at room temperature for at least 1 and up to 2 hours until completely softened. Efforts to speed the softening by microwaving the cheese can result in melted, and not softened, cheese. So plan ahead!

# peanut butter and chocolate cheesecake cups

These sweet morsels may be small, but they are loaded with goodness. They may remind you of your favorite peanut and chocolate candy bar, with much less sugar and fat, of course. As an optional garnish, melt 2 ounces regular or sugar-free chocolate and drizzle it over the top of each cooled cup. You'll need mini-muffin foil baking liners, available in well-stocked supermarkets, to make these.

### Crust

**2 cups chocolate wafer crumbs (about 36 cookies)**

**¼ cup SPLENDA® No Calorie Sweetener, Granulated**

**5 tablespoons light butter, melted**

### Peanut Butter Filling

**½ cup SPLENDA® No Calorie Sweetener, Granulated**

**3 tablespoons reduced-fat peanut butter**

**3 tablespoons reduced-fat cream cheese, softened (see page 117)**

### Chocolate Cheesecake Filling

**4 ounces unsweetened chocolate, finely chopped**

**One 8-ounce package reduced-fat cream cheese, softened**

**1¾ cups SPLENDA® No Calorie Sweetener, Granulated**

**½ cup nonfat milk**

**½ cup liquid egg substitute**

**1 teaspoon vanilla extract**

1. Position a rack in the center of the oven and preheat to 350°F. Place 24 mini-muffin foil baking cups on a baking sheet.

2. To make the crust, mix the cookie crumbs, SPLENDA® Granulated Sweetener, and melted butter in a medium bowl until the crumbs are evenly moistened.

3. To make the peanut butter filling, mash the SPLENDA® Granulated Sweetener, peanut butter, and cream cheese in a small bowl with a rubber spatula until blended.

4. To make the chocolate cheesecake filling, melt the chocolate in a small stainless steel or glass heatproof bowl over (but not touching) a small saucepan of simmering water until the chocolate is melted. Remove the bowl from the saucepan and cool the chocolate until lukewarm.

> CONTINUED

**5.** Beat the cream cheese in a medium bowl with an electric mixer on medium speed until creamy, scraping down the sides of the bowl often. Gradually add the SPLENDA® Granulated Sweetener and beat until smooth, scraping down the sides of the bowl. Gradually beat in the milk. On low speed, beat in the melted and cooled chocolate, then the egg substitute and vanilla, mixing until well blended, again scraping down the sides of the bowl as needed.

**6.** Divide the crumb mixture evenly among the cups and firmly press the crumbs into the bottom of each cup. Spoon an equal amount (about ½ teaspoon) of the peanut butter filling into each cup. Divide the cheesecake filling among the cups.

**7.** Bake until the filling feels just set when pressed lightly, about 12 minutes.

**8.** Let cool completely on the baking sheet. Cover with plastic wrap and refrigerate until chilled, at least 2 hours. Serve chilled or at room temperature.

Cheesecakes are perfect for entertaining because they must be prepared a few hours before serving. That's one course that you'll have well out of the way before company arrives.

# raspberry cheese tartlets

At first glance, these individual cheesecakes look like pristine bites of the familiar classic variety. But when diners cut into them, they find a fresh raspberry surprise. You can also make them with fresh blueberries. Using foil liners in muffin cups makes them easy to assemble.

### Crust

¾ cup graham cracker crumbs
   (see page 127)

3 tablespoons light margarine, melted

2 tablespoons SPLENDA® No Calorie
   Sweetener, Granulated

1 cup fresh raspberries

### Filling

4 ounces reduced-fat cream cheese,
   softened (see page 117)

½ cup plain nonfat yogurt

1 cup SPLENDA® No Calorie Sweetener,
   Granulated

½ cup liquid egg substitute

#### NUTRITIONAL INFORMATION

Serving Size: 1 tartlet
Total Calories: 120
Calories from Fat: 45
Total Fat: 5 g
Saturated Fat: 2 g
Cholesterol: 5 mg

Sodium: 160 mg
Total Carbohydrates: 15 g
Dietary Fiber: 0 g
Sugars: 4 g
Protein: 1 g

**EXCHANGES PER SERVING**
1 starch, 1 fat

1. Position a rack in the center of the oven and preheat to 350°F. Line 10 muffin cups with foil liners.

2. To make the crust, mix the graham cracker crumbs, melted margarine, and SPLENDA® Granulated Sweetener in a medium bowl until the crumbs are evenly moistened. Press 1 tablespoon of the mixture into the bottom of each cup. Arrange 4 or 5 raspberries in each cup.

3. To make the filling, beat the cream cheese in a medium bowl with an electric mixer on medium speed until creamy. Add the yogurt and beat, scraping down the sides of the bowl often, until smooth. Beat in the SPLENDA® Granulated Sweetener and egg substitute, until well blended. Spoon the filling into the cups, dividing it evenly.

4. Bake just until the centers feel firm to the touch when lightly pressed, 15 to 20 minutes.

5. Let cool completely in the pan on a wire rack. Cover with plastic wrap and refrigerate until chilled, at least 2 hours. Serve chilled.

# dulce de leche cheesecake

*Dulce de leche,* made from long-cooked sweetened milk, is the ultimate caramel sauce. A specialty of South American cuisine, you'll find domestic and imported versions at Latino grocers and many supermarkets.

### Crust

**Nonstick cooking spray for the pan**

**1 cup graham cracker or vanilla wafer crumbs (see page 127)**

**3 tablespoons unsalted butter, melted**

### Filling

**Three 8-ounce packages reduced-fat cream cheese, softened (see page 117)**

**1 cup SPLENDA® No Calorie Sweetener, Granulated**

**2 tablespoons all-purpose flour**

**2 teaspoons vanilla extract**

**3 large eggs, at room temperature**

**⅓ cup 2% reduced-fat milk**

**½ cup *dulce de leche* such as Nestlé La Lechera sweetened condensed milk**

---

**NUTRITIONAL INFORMATION**

Serving Size: 1 slice
Total Calories: 190
Calories from Fat: 110
Total Fat: 12 g
Saturated Fat: 7 g
Cholesterol: 70 mg

Sodium: 200 mg
Total Carbohydrates: 15 g
Dietary Fiber: 0 g
Sugars: 9 g
Protein: 7 g

**EXCHANGES PER SERVING**
1 starch, 2 fats

---

1. Position a rack in the center of the oven and preheat to 400 °F. Lightly spray the inside of a 9-inch springform pan with the cooking spray.

2. To make the crust, mix the crumbs and melted butter in a medium bowl until the crumbs are evenly moistened. Press the crumb mixture evenly into the bottom of the prepared pan.

3. Bake until the crust is lightly browned, about 10 minutes. Let cool on a wire rack while you make the filling. Reduce the oven temperature to 325°F.

4. To make the filling, beat the cream cheese, SPLENDA® Granulated Sweetener, and flour in a large bowl with an electric mixer on medium speed, scraping down the sides of the bowl often, until creamy, about 2 minutes. Beat in the vanilla. One at a time, beat in the eggs, mixing just until each one is incorporated. Beat in the milk until the mixture is smooth.

5. Transfer ½ cup of the batter to a small bowl. Add the *dulce de leche* and whisk until combined. Pour the plain batter into the cooled crust. Place a dollop of the *dulce de leche* batter on the top. Insert a butter knife into the batter and swirl the two batters together for a marbling effect.

6. Bake until the sides of the filling are slightly puffed and the center is almost set, 45 to 55 minutes.

7. Transfer the cheesecake to a wire cake rack. Run a knife around the inside of the pan to release the cheesecake. Cool completely. Cover with plastic wrap and refrigerate until chilled, at least 8 hours or overnight. To serve, remove the sides of the pan. Cut into wedges with a sharp, wet knife and serve chilled.

# mocha swirl cheesecake

Instant espresso powder and hot-chocolate mix make it easy as pie (or cheesecake?) to crank up the flavor of your cheesecake a notch or two. The sophisticated mocha taste will be best appreciated by grownups, so consider this lovely dessert as the finale to a dinner party.

### Crust

**Nonstick cooking spray for the pan**

**2 cups chocolate wafers (about 44 wafers), crushed**

**¼ cup SPLENDA® No Calorie Sweetener, Granulated**

**4 tablespoons unsalted butter, melted**

**2 tablespoons unsweetened cocoa powder**

1. Position a rack in the center of the oven and preheat to 400°F. Lightly spray the inside of a 9-inch springform pan with the cooking spray.

2. To make the crust, mix the cookie crumbs, SPLENDA® Granulated Sweetener, melted butter, and cocoa powder in a medium bowl until the crumbs are evenly moistened. Press the crumb mixture evenly into the bottom of the prepared pan.

3. Bake until the edges of the crust cook crisp, about 10 minutes. Let cool on a wire rack while making the filling. Reduce the oven temperature to 325°F.

## Filling

Three 8-ounce packages reduced-fat
    cream cheese, softened (see page 117)

¾ cup SPLENDA® No Calorie Sweetener,
    Granulated

2 large eggs plus 2 large egg whites,
    at room temperature

1½ tablespoons cornstarch

¼ teaspoon salt

¾ cup reduced-fat sour cream

2 teaspoons vanilla extract

1¼ teaspoons instant espresso

Two .55-ounce envelopes sugar-free
    instant cocoa mix

### NUTRITIONAL INFORMATION

Serving Size: 1 slice
Total Calories: 210
Calories from Fat: 120
Total Fat: 13 g
Saturated Fat: 8 g
Cholesterol: 60 mg

Sodium: 280 mg
Total Carbohydrates: 16 g
Dietary Fiber: 0 g
Sugars: 8 g
Protein: 7 g

EXCHANGES PER SERVING
1 starch, 1 medium fat
meat, 1 fat

4. To make the filling, beat the cream cheese and SPLENDA® Granulated Sweetener in a large bowl with an electric mixer on medium speed, scraping down the sides of the bowl often, until creamy, about 2 minutes. Add the eggs, egg whites, cornstarch, and salt and beat just until blended. Add the sour cream and vanilla and beat just until incorporated.

5. Transfer ½ cup of the batter to a small bowl. Add the instant espresso and cocoa mix and whisk until combined. Spread half of the plain batter in the cooled crust. Place half of the mocha batter on the top. Insert a butter knife into the batter and swirl the two batters together for a marbling effect. Top with the remaining plain batter. Add dollops of the remaining mocha batter and swirl the batters together again.

6. Bake until the sides of the filling are slightly puffed and the center is almost set, 45 to 55 minutes.

7. Transfer to a wire rack and run a knife around the inside of the pan to release the cheesecake. Let cool completely. Cover with plastic wrap and refrigerate until well chilled, at least 8 hours or overnight.

8. To serve, remove the sides of the pan. Cut the cheesecake into wedges with a sharp, wet knife and serve chilled.

An overbaked cheesecake is more likely to crack than one that has been baked just until the center is almost, but not quite set. The center will firm with chilling. Another sign of doneness in cheesecake is when the sides of the batter are puffed and lightly browned.

# mango cheesecake

The exotic taste of mango infuses this wonderful, velvety cheesecake with tropical flavor. The mangoes should be fragrant and fully ripe, yielding somewhat when squeezed. If you'd like to garnish the cheesecake, use sliced mango, kiwi, and strawberries for a bright mélange of colors.

### Crust

**Nonstick cooking spray for the pan**

**1½ cups graham cracker crumbs (see facing page)**

**5 tablespoons unsalted butter, melted**

**¼ cup SPLENDA® Sugar Blend**

### Filling

**3 large ripe mangoes, peeled, pitted, and chopped (3 cups, see page 83)**

**Three 8-ounce packages reduced-fat cream cheese, softened (see page 117)**

**2 tablespoons plus ⅔ cup SPLENDA® Sugar Blend, divided**

**½ teaspoon almond extract**

**4 large eggs, at room temperature**

1. Position a rack in the center of the oven and preheat to 325°F. Lightly spray the inside of a 9-inch springform pan with the cooking spray.

2. To make the crust, mix the graham cracker crumbs, melted butter, and SPLENDA® Sugar Blend in a medium bowl until the crumbs are evenly moistened. Press the crumb mixture evenly into the bottom and ½ inch up the sides of the prepared pan. Bake until the edges of the crust look crisp, about 12 minutes.

3. To make the filling, purée the mango and the 2 tablespoons of SPLENDA® Sugar Blend in a blender or food processor. You should have about 2 cups purée.

NUTRITIONAL INFORMATION

Serving Size: 1 slice
Total Calories: 300
Calories from Fat: 180
Total Fat: 20 g
Saturated Fat: 12 g
Cholesterol: 125 mg

Sodium: 360 mg
Total Carbohydrates: 21 g
Dietary Fiber: 1 g
Sugars: 13 g
Protein: 9 g

EXCHANGES PER SERVING
1½ starches, 1 medium
fat meat, 3 fats

4. Beat the cream cheese in a large bowl with an electric mixer on medium speed until creamy. Gradually beat in the remaining ⅔ cup SPLENDA®, then the almond extract, and mix, scraping down the sides of the bowl often, until the mixture is smooth. One at a time, beat in the eggs, mixing just until each one is incorporated. Add the mango purée and mix just until blended. Pour into the crust and smooth the top.

5. Bake until the sides of the filling are slightly puffed and the center is almost set, about 1 hour, 20 minutes to 1 hour, 30 minutes.

6. Transfer to a wire rack and let cool completely. Cover with plastic wrap and refrigerate until chilled, at least 3 hours or overnight.

7. To serve, run a knife around the inside of the pan to release the cheesecake. Remove the sides of the pan. Cut into wedges with a sharp, wet knife and serve chilled.

You can find graham cracker and vanilla wafer crumbs in the baking aisle of well-stocked supermarkets, or make your own in a blender or a food processor fitted with the metal blade: Coarsely crumble the crackers first, then work in batches to get the crumbs to finer, uniform crumbs. Or, use the low tech method: Crumble the crackers by hand in a zippered plastic bag and then crush to fine crumbs with a rolling pin. Nine whole graham crackers make about 1⅓ cups crumbs.

# ricotta cheesecake

This luxuriously textured cheesecake, is based on the Italian *torta di ricotta*. Made in a food processor, it comes together in a snap, yielding a thin, rich dessert, not the towering American type of cheesecake.

### Crust

1 cup graham cracker crumbs
(see page 127)

4 tablespoons unsalted butter, melted

3 tablespoons SPLENDA® No Calorie Sweetener, Granulated

### Filling

12 ounces reduced-fat cream cheese, softened (1½ eight-ounce packages, see page 117)

1 cup part-skim ricotta cheese, at room temperature

½ cup SPLENDA® No Calorie Sweetener, Granulated

½ cup liquid egg substitute

2 tablespoons unsalted butter, melted

2 tablespoons fresh orange juice

1 teaspoon grated orange zest

1 tablespoon fresh lemon juice

1½ teaspoons vanilla extract

**1.** Position a rack in the center of the oven and preheat to 350°F. Lightly spray the inside of a 9-inch springform pan with nonstick cooking spray.

**2.** To make the crust, mix the graham cracker crumbs, melted butter, and SPLENDA® Granulated Sweetener in a medium bowl until the crumbs are evenly moistened. Press the crumb mixture evenly into the bottom of the prepared pan.

**3.** To make the filling, combine the cream cheese, ricotta, SPLENDA® Granulated Sweetener, egg substitute, melted butter, orange juice and zest, lemon juice, and vanilla in a food processor. Process until the mixture is very smooth, stopping to scrape down the sides of the bowl often, about 3 minutes. Pour into the crust and smooth the top.

**4.** Bake until the center of the filling feels almost set, 25 to 30 minutes. Turn the oven off, let stand in oven 30 minutes with door partially opened to cool.

**5.** Transfer to a wire rack and let cool completely. Cover with plastic wrap and refrigerate until well chilled, at least 3 hours.

**6.** To serve, run a knife around the inside of the pan to release the cheesecake. Remove the sides of the pan. Cut into wedges with a sharp, wet knife and serve chilled.

### NUTRITIONAL INFORMATION

Serving Size: 1 slice
Total Calories: 230
Calories from Fat: 150
Total Fat: 17 g
Saturated Fat: 10 g
Cholesterol: 50 mg
Sodium: 300 mg

Total Carbohydrates: 11 g
Dietary Fiber: 0 g
Sugars: 4 g
Protein: 8 g

**EXCHANGES PER SERVING**
½ starch, 1 medium fat meat, 2 fats

fruit desserts

# sour cream–apple crumble

This satisfying dessert, with its sweet-tart filling of apples and sour cream and a nutty streusel topping, is reminiscent of something that you might be served from an Amish or Pennsylvania Dutch kitchen. You'll want to serve it warm from of the oven—its aroma is so enticing that you won't be able to wait until it cools, anyway!

### Filling

**Nonstick cooking spray for the pan**

**3 Golden Delicious apples, peeled, cored, sliced into ½-inch thick slices (see page 132)**

**2 teaspoons fresh lemon juice**

**1½ teaspoons apple pie spice (see Note)**

**½ cup plus 2 tablespoons SPLENDA® No Calorie Sweetener, Granulated**

**½ cup all-purpose baking mix such as Bisquick mix**

**½ cup sour cream**

**2 large eggs, lightly beaten**

**1 tablespoon unsalted butter, at room temperature**

**1 teaspoon vanilla extract**

**¼ teaspoon almond extract**

1. Position a rack in the center of the oven and preheat to 350°F. Lightly spray the inside of a 9-inch round deep-dish pie pan with the cooking spray.

2. To make the filling, mix the apples, lemon juice, and apple pie spice in a medium bowl. Spread in the pie pan. Whisk the SPLENDA® Granulated Sweetener, baking mix, sour cream, eggs, butter, and vanilla and almond extracts until smooth. Pour over the apples.

## Topping

½ cup all-purpose baking mix such as Bisquick mix

⅓ cup SPLENDA® No Calorie Sweetener, Granulated

3 tablespoons unsalted butter, chilled, thinly sliced

⅓ cup chopped pecans

Freshly grated nutmeg for garnish

NUTRITIONAL INFORMATION

Serving Size: 1 slice
Total Calories: 230
Calories from Fat: 140
Total Fat: 16 g
Saturated Fat: 7 g
Cholesterol: 75 mg

Sodium: 220 mg
Total Carbohydrates: 19 g
Dietary Fiber: 1 g
Sugars: 5 g
Protein: 4 g

EXCHANGES PER SERVING
1½ starches, 3 fats

3. To make the topping, combine the baking mix and SPLENDA® Granulated Sweetener in a medium bowl. Add the butter. Using a pastry blender, two knives, or an electric mixer on low speed, cut the butter into the dry ingredients until the mixture resembles coarse crumbs. Stir in the pecans. Sprinkle over the filling.

4. Bake until the filling is set and the topping is golden brown and crisp, 40 to 45 minutes. Let cool for 5 minutes, then cut into wedges and serve warm, sprinkled with nutmeg.

NOTE: To make your own apple pie spice, mix ¾ teaspoon ground cinnamon with ¼ teaspoon each ground allspice, ground ginger, and ground nutmeg, and ⅛ teaspoon ground cloves.

# crispy apple crisp

There are many apple crisps, but few can claim that a topping is truly crisp. This one sports a mixture of oats, rice cereal, and walnuts, tossed with spicy syrup that bakes into a glossy glaze.

## Filling

**Nonstick cooking spray for the pan**

**1 cup SPLENDA® No Calorie Sweetener, Granulated**

**1 teaspoon ground cinnamon**

**1 teaspoon orange zest**

**¼ cup orange juice**

**5 Golden Delicious apples, peeled, cored, cut into ½-inch thick slices**

## Topping

**1 cup old-fashioned rolled oats**

**2 tablespoons SPLENDA® No Calorie Sweetener, Granulated**

**¼ teaspoon ground cinnamon**

**2 tablespoons unsalted butter, diced**

**½ cup crisp rice cereal**

**½ cup chopped walnuts**

1. Position a rack in the center of the oven and preheat to 350°F. Lightly spray the inside of an 8-inch square baking dish with the cooking spray.

2. To make the filling, whisk together the SPLENDA® Granulated Sweetener, cinnamon, orange zest, and orange juice in a large bowl. Add the apples and toss gently. Spread into the baking dish.

3. To make the topping, mix the oats, SPLENDA®, and cinnamon in a medium bowl. Add the butter. Using a pastry blender or two knives, cut the butter into the dry ingredients until the mixture is crumbly. Stir in the cereal and walnuts. Scatter over the apples.

4. Bake until the apples are tender and the topping is lightly browned, about 45 minutes. Let cool for 5 minutes, then cut into squares and serve warm.

Different fruit varieties work best for different recipes. All-purpose apples that hold their shape after cooking include Golden Delicious and Granny Smith. Bosc pears will not fall apart when baked and are the ones to use for baked or poached pears. Crisps and crumbles, on the other hand, are best with sweet, juicy types like Bartletts. Use the suggestions in the ingredients lists for the best choices. (1 Golden Delicious apple, peeled, cored, and sliced into ½-inch thick slices will yield about 1 cup. 1 ripe Bartlett pear will yield about ¾ cup.)

### NUTRITIONAL INFORMATION

Serving Size: 1 square
Total Calories: 190
Calories from Fat: 80
Total Fat: 9 g
Saturated Fat: 2.5 g
Cholesterol: 10 mg

Sodium: 15 mg
Total Carbohydrates: 27 g
Dietary Fiber: 3 g
Sugars: 10 g
Protein: 3 g

EXCHANGES PER SERVING
1 starch, 1 fruit, 2 fats

# baked apples with orange-cinnamon sauce

Sometimes the simplest pleasures are the best. With just a handful of ingredients, you can have apples ready for the oven in just a few minutes. Warm and tender, baked apples are great for brunch or dessert, or even as a side dish for pork or baked ham.

**Nonstick cooking spray for the pan**

**1½ cups freshly squeezed orange juice**

**⅔ cup SPLENDA® No Calorie Sweetener, Granulated**

**½ teaspoon ground cinnamon**

**1½ tablespoons all-purpose flour**

**2 tablespoons unsalted butter**

**2 teaspoons grated orange zest**

**8 small Granny Smith or other cooking apples (about 5 ounces each)**

### NUTRITIONAL INFORMATION

Serving Size: 1 apple with sauce

Total Calories: 90

Calories from Fat: 25

Total Fat: 3 g

Saturated Fat: 2 g

Cholesterol: 10 mg

Sodium: 0 mg

Total Carbohydrates: 17 g

Dietary Fiber: 1 g

Sugars: 11 g

Protein: 1 g

**EXCHANGES PER SERVING**

1 fruit, 1 fat

1. Position a rack in the center of the oven and preheat to 350°F. Lightly spray an 11-by-8½-inch baking dish with the cooking spray.

2. Combine the orange juice, SPLENDA® Granulated Sweetener, and cinnamon in a medium saucepan. Sprinkle in the flour and whisk to dissolve. Bring to a boil over medium heat and cook, whisking often, until the sauce thickens slightly. Remove from the heat and whisk in the butter and orange zest.

3. Core the apples. Peel the top 1 inch of peel from each apple. Place the apples in the baking dish. Pour the sauce over the apples.

4. Bake, uncovered, basting every 10 minutes with the juices in the dish, until the apples are tender when pierced with the tip of a sharp knife, 35 to 40 minutes. Serve each apple in a bowl, topped with a spoonful of the sauce.

# double-crust peach cobbler

Cobblers are by nature easy desserts, made from seasonal fruit "cobbled" together with some kind of a crust. But timing can be tricky to coordinate the doneness of the components. This recipe uses a few tricks to ensure crisp bottom and top crusts and tender, juicy peaches.

**Nonstick cooking spray for the pan**

**5 pounds ripe peaches**

**¼ cup pineapple juice**

**¼ cup all-purpose flour**

**1¾ cups SPLENDA® No Calorie Sweetener, Granulated**

**2 tablespoons unsalted butter**

**½ teaspoon almond extract**

**2 refrigerated 9-inch piecrusts (one 15-ounce package)**

### NUTRITIONAL INFORMATION

| | |
|---|---|
| Serving Size: 1 square | Sodium: 190 mg |
| Total Calories: 330 | Total Carbohydrates: 46 g |
| Calories from Fat: 140 | Dietary Fiber: 3 g |
| Total Fat: 15 g | Sugars: 18 g |
| Saturated Fat: 7 g | Protein: 4 g |
| Cholesterol: 15 mg | EXCHANGES PER SERVING |
| | 1 starch, 2 fruits, 3 fats |

1. Position a rack in the center of the oven and preheat to 450°F. Lightly spray an 11-by-8½-inch baking dish with the cooking spray.

2. Bring a large pot of water to a boil over high heat. A few at a time, drop the peaches into the water and cook until the skin begins to loosen, 15 to 30 seconds. Using a slotted spoon, transfer the peaches to a large bowl of iced water. Using a sharp knife, peel, pit, and cut the peaches into ½-inch-thick slices. You should have 10 cups sliced peaches.

3. Whisk the pineapple juice and flour in a small bowl to dissolve the flour, and pour into a large saucepan. Add the peaches, SPLENDA® Granulated Sweetener, and butter. Bring to a boil over medium heat, stirring occasionally. Remove from the heat and stir in the almond extract. Let stand while baking the bottom crust.

4. Unroll 1 piecrust onto a lightly floured work surface. Trim the dough to an 11-by-8½-inch rectangle and place in the baking dish; discard the dough scraps. Pierce the dough in several places with a fork. Bake until the crust is lightly browned, 10 to 12 minutes. Remove from the oven. Spread the peach filling in the dish.

5. Unroll the remaining piecrust on the work surface and cut the dough into 1-inch-wide strips. Arrange the strips on the filling in a lattice pattern. Bake until the top crust is lightly browned, about 15 minutes. Let cool for 5 minutes, then cut into squares and serve warm.

# maple-baked pears
## with vanilla frozen yogurt

For a light ending to a fine meal, these pears, baked and served with an orange and maple flavored syrup, are hard to surpass. They are excellent with frozen vanilla yogurt, on their own, or serve them with crisp cookies alongside.

**Nonstick cooking spray for the pan**

**4 ripe Bosc pears**

**¼ cup SPLENDA® No Calorie Sweetener, Granulated**

**2 tablespoons fresh lemon juice**

**2 tablespoons unsalted butter, melted**

**¼ teaspoon ground cinnamon**

**¼ teaspoon maple extract**

**½ cup fresh orange juice**

**1 pint low-fat frozen vanilla yogurt for serving**

1. Position a rack in the center of the oven and preheat to 375°F. Lightly spray the inside of an 11-by-7-inch baking dish with the cooking spray.

2. Peel the pears. Cut each pear in half lengthwise and scoop out the core with a melon baller or the tip of a swivel-blade vegetable peeler. Place the pears, cut side down, in the dish.

3. Mix the SPLENDA® Granulated Sweetener, lemon juice, melted butter, cinnamon, and maple extract in a small bowl. Spoon the mixture over the pears. Turn the pears to coat them on both sides with the cinnamon mixture, replacing them cut side down. Pour the orange juice around the pears.

4. Bake, uncovered, basting every 10 minutes with the juices in the dish, until the pears are tender when pierced with the tip of a small sharp knife, 40 to 45 minutes. Serve warm or cooled to room temperature, with a small scoop of the yogurt, and drizzled with the pan juices.

### NUTRITIONAL INFORMATION

Serving Size: 1 pear half with sauce and yogurt
Total Calories: 150
Calories from Fat: 35
Total Fat: 3.5 g
Saturated Fat: 2.5 g
Cholesterol: 20 mg
Sodium: 35 mg
Total Carbohydrates: 28 g
Dietary Fiber: 3 g
Sugars: 18 g
Protein: 2 g

**EXCHANGES PER SERVING**
1 starch, 1 fruit, 1 fat

# *easy pear crisp*

The next time you'd like a warm autumn fruit crisp, try this for a change. Graham crackers make this the easiest crisp topping of all and Bartlett pears, which are especially juicy, are a welcome alternative to apples. A food processor makes quick work of processing the topping ingredients into coarse crumbs.

## *Filling*

**Nonstick cooking spray for the pan**

**4 ripe Bosc or Bartlett pears, peeled, cored, cut into ½-inch-thick slices (see page 132)**

**¼ cup SPLENDA® No Calorie Sweetener, Granulated**

**3 tablespoons water**

**2 tablespoons all-purpose flour**

**1 tablespoon fresh lemon juice**

**½ teaspoon ground cinnamon**

## *Topping*

**3 whole graham crackers, coarsely crumbled**

**¼ cup SPLENDA® No Calorie Sweetener, Granulated**

**4 tablespoons light butter**

**2 tablespoons all-purpose flour**

**1 teaspoon ground cinnamon**

1. Position a rack in the center of the oven and preheat to 350°F. Lightly spray the inside of an 8-inch square baking dish with the cooking spray.

2. To make the filling, mix the pears, SPLENDA® Granulated Sweetener, water, flour, lemon juice, and cinnamon in a medium bowl. Spread in the baking dish.

3. To make the topping, combine the graham crackers, SPLENDA® Granulated Sweetener, butter, flour, and cinnamon in a food processor. Pulse until the mixture is crumbly. Sprinkle over the pears.

4. Bake until the pear juices are bubbling, 40 to 45 minutes. Let cool for 5 minutes, then cut into squares and serve warm.

When cooking with fresh fruit, use ripe fruits in season. No amount of sweetening will improve poor-tasting produce.

### NUTRITIONAL INFORMATION

Serving Size: 1 square
Total Calories: 120
Calories from Fat: 35
Total Fat: 4.5 g
Saturated Fat: 2.5 g
Cholesterol: 15 mg

Sodium: 60 mg
Total Carbohydrates: 21 g
Dietary Fiber: 3 g
Sugars: 8 g
Protein: 2 g

EXCHANGES PER SERVING
½ starch, 1 fruit, 1 fat

custards, puddings, and
other spoon desserts

# almond-coconut flan

Flan, the Spanish version of baked custard, is always coated with caramel. But the custard itself is subject to variation, here with coconut and almond flavors. Instead of individual cups, the custard is baked into a large round, which makes for easy serving. Toasted almonds and coconut make nice garnishes.

½ cup plus ⅓ cup **SPLENDA**®
  **Sugar Blend, divided**

**2 tablespoons water**

**One 13½-ounce can unsweetened
  coconut milk**

**1½ cups 1% low-fat milk**

**3 large eggs and 3 large egg yolks,
  at room temperature**

**¾ cup sweetened flaked coconut**

**½ teaspoon almond extract**

**½ cup sliced almonds, toasted
  (see Note, page 96)**

1. Position a rack in the center of the oven and preheat to 350°F.

2. Combine ½ cup of the SPLENDA® Sugar Blend and the water in a small, heavy-bottomed saucepan. Cook over medium heat, stirring constantly, just until the SPLENDA® dissolves. Continue to cook without stirring, occasionally swirling the pot by the handle to combine the ingredients, until the caramel is golden brown. Working quickly and protecting your hands with long oven mitts or kitchen towels, immediately pour the caramel into a 9-inch round cake pan and tilt the pan to coat as much of the bottom and sides as possible with caramel. The caramel will harden and may crack.

3. Combine the coconut milk and milk in a medium saucepan and bring to a simmer over medium heat.

4. Combine the remaining ⅓ cup SPLENDA® with the whole eggs and egg yolks in a blender and blend on high speed for 15 seconds. With the blender on, pour the hot milk mixture in a slow steady stream through the feed hole in the blender lid. Add the coconut and almond extract and blend until smooth. Pour into the caramel-coated pan. Place the pan in a larger, shallow roasting pan or baking dish.

5. Place the roasting pan with the cake pan in the oven. Carefully pour enough hot water to come halfway up the sides of the cake pan. Bake until a knife inserted in the center of the custard comes out clean, about 45 minutes.

6. Carefully remove the cake pan from the water, transfer to a wire rack, and let cool for 30 minutes. Cover the custard with plastic wrap, pressing the plastic directly on the surface to prevent a skin from forming, (see page 143) and refrigerate until well chilled, at least 8 hours or overnight.

7. To serve, run a thin knife around the edges of the pan to release the custard. Invert the pan onto a rimmed serving platter. Holding the pan and platter together, give them a sharp shake to dislodge the custard from the pan, and remove the pan. Sprinkle with toasted almonds. Cut into wedges and serve chilled.

# cuban rice pudding

This ultra-creamy Hispanic version of rice pudding is simmered in a saucepan, not baked. Use a heavy-bottomed saucepan and stir often to prevent scorching. You can personalize it by replacing the raisins with a quarter-cup or so of currants or dried cherries along with the milk, but note that this will slightly alter the nutritional information. It is best served warm, but it can also be chilled.

**2 cups water**

**1 cup long-grain rice**

**¼ teaspoon salt**

**3 cups 2% reduced-fat milk**

**½ cup SPLENDA® No Calorie Sweetener, Granulated**

**⅛ teaspoon ground cinnamon**

**¼ cup raisins**

**1½ teaspoons vanilla extract**

**1.** Bring the water to a boil in a medium, heavy-bottomed saucepan over high heat. Stir in the rice and salt and return to a boil. Cover tightly and reduce the heat to low. Simmer until the rice is very tender and all of the water has been absorbed, about 35 minutes.

**2.** Stir in the milk, SPLENDA® Granulated Sweetener, cinnamon, and raisins and bring to a simmer over medium heat, stirring occasionally. Reduce the heat to low. Simmer, uncovered, gently stirring occasionally (do not break up the rice grains), until the milk is absorbed, about 20 minutes. Remove from the heat and stir in the vanilla.

**3.** To serve, spoon into individual bowls and serve warm.

### NUTRITIONAL INFORMATION

Serving Size: ½ cup
Total Calories: 150
Calories from Fat: 20
Total Fat: 2 g
Saturated Fat: 1 g
Cholesterol: 5 mg

Sodium: 115 mg
Total Carbohydrates: 28 g
Dietary Fiber: 0 g
Sugars: 7 g
Protein: 5 g

**EXCHANGES PER SERVING**
1½ starches, 1 reduced-fat milk

# banana pudding

All over the South, restaurants serve up countless portions of banana pudding, that sinful concoction of vanilla pudding, vanilla wafers, ripe bananas, and plenty of whipped cream. With just a few savvy exchanges of ingredients, you can make this version, which is every bit as good—but you'll have to find something else to feel guilty about.

**2 cups 1% low-fat milk**

**⅓ cup SPLENDA® No Calorie Sweetener, Granulated**

**3 tablespoons cornstarch**

**1 large egg**

**¼ teaspoon salt**

**1 tablespoon unsalted butter**

**1 teaspoon vanilla extract**

**24 reduced-fat vanilla wafers**

**2 ripe bananas, thinly sliced**

**Reduced-fat frozen whipped topping, thawed, for garnish**

### NUTRITIONAL INFORMATION

Serving Size: 1 pudding
   with whipped topping
   (¼ recipe)
Total Calories: 270
Calories from Fat: 60
Total Fat: 7g
Saturated Fat: 3g
Cholesterol: 65 mg

Sodium: 230 mg
Total Carbohydrates: 45 g
Dietary Fiber: 2 g
Sugars: 21 g
Protein: 7 g

**EXCHANGES PER SERVING**
2½ starches, ½ reduced-
   fat milk

1. In a medium, heavy-bottomed saucepan, whisk the milk, SPLENDA® Granulated Sweetener, cornstarch, egg, and salt until well combined. Cook over medium heat, whisking constantly, until the mixture thickens and comes to a full boil. Remove from the heat. Add the butter and vanilla and stir until the butter dissolves.

2. Coarsely crumble 2 vanilla wafers into each of four 1-cup dessert cups. Divide half of the banana slices among the cups, top with half of the pudding and 8 more cookies. Repeat with the remaining bananas and pudding (reserving the remaining cookies), being sure that the bananas are completely covered with the pudding to avoid discoloring. Cover each pudding with plastic wrap, pressing the wrap directly on the surface of the pudding; poke a few holes in the plastic wrap with the tip of a small knife to allow the steam to escape. Refrigerate until chilled, at least 2 hours.

3. Top each pudding with a dollop of whipped topping and 2 wafers. Serve chilled.

A tough "skin" forms on cornstarch-based and other puddings during chilling. While some people love this layer, others don't. To prevent the skin from forming, press a sheet of plastic wrap or waxed paper directly on the surface of the hot pudding. Poke a few holes in the plastic wrap with the tip of a sharp knife to allow the steam to escape. The wrap keeps out the air, which is an instrumental element in the skin formation.

# crème caramel

These classics of French cuisine are rich with eggs and cloaked with golden brown caramel. Because they must be made well ahead of serving to firm and chill before unmolding, they are perfect dinner party fare, as you can prepare them the night before or early in the day and be free to attend to your other cooking. Garnish each custard with a few berries and a mint sprig, if you wish.

**Nonstick cooking spray for the custard cups**

**1 cup SPLENDA® Sugar Blend, divided**

**3 tablespoons water**

**2 large eggs plus 2 large egg yolks**

**2½ cups whole milk**

**Pinch of salt**

**1 tablespoon vanilla extract**

### NUTRITIONAL INFORMATION

Serving Size: 1 custard
Total Calories: 240
Calories from Fat: 60
Total Fat: 6 g
Saturated Fat: 3 g
Cholesterol: 150 mg

Sodium: 115 mg
Total Carbohydrates: 38 g
Dietary Fiber: 0 g
Sugars: 37 g
Protein: 6 g

**EXCHANGES PER SERVING**
2 starches, ½ low-fat
milk, 1 fat

**1.** Position a rack in the center of the oven and preheat to 325°F. Lightly spray the insides of six 6-ounce custard cups or ramekins with the cooking spray.

**2.** Combine ½ cup of the SPLENDA® Sugar Blend and the water in a small, heavy-bottomed saucepan. Cook over medium heat, stirring constantly, just until the SPLENDA® dissolves. Continue to cook without stirring, occasionally swirling the pot by the handle to combine the ingredients, until the caramel is golden brown. Working quickly, immediately pour the caramel into the bottom of the custard cups, dividing it evenly.

**3.** Whisk the whole eggs and egg yolks in a medium bowl until blended. Whisk in the milk, the remaining ½ cup SPLENDA®, the salt, and the vanilla. Divide among the custard cups. Place the cups in a shallow roasting pan or baking dish.

> CONTINUED

**4.** Place the roasting pan with the cups in the oven. Carefully pour enough hot water to come 1 inch up the sides of the cups. Bake until a knife inserted in the center of a custard comes out clean, about 50 minutes.

**5.** Carefully remove the cups from the water, transfer to a wire rack, and let cool for 30 minutes. Cover each custard with plastic wrap, pressing the plastic directly on the surface to prevent a skin from forming (see page 143), and refrigerate until well chilled, at least 4 hours or overnight.

**6.** To serve, loosen the edges of each custard with a knife. One at a time, invert a cup onto a dessert plate. Holding the cup and plate together, give them a sharp shake to unmold the custard from the cup, and remove the cup. Serve chilled.

# bread pudding with raisins

For the best bread pudding, start with day-old, crusty French or Italian bread. The firm textures of these breads allow them to soak up the sweet custard without becoming soggy. If you have the desire for bread pudding but don't have day-old bread, bake cubed, fresh bread in a preheated 350°F oven for 20 minutes or so, until it crisps around the edges without browning, let cool, and proceed with the recipe.

**2¼ cups 1% low-fat milk**

**1½ cups SPLENDA® No Calorie Sweetener, Granulated**

**2 large eggs**

**1½ teaspoons ground cinnamon**

**1 teaspoon vanilla extract**

**5 cups cubed day-old French or Italian bread (½- to 1-inch cubes)**

**½ cup raisins**

1. Position a rack in the center of the oven and preheat to 350°F.

2. Whisk the milk, SPLENDA® Granulated Sweetener, eggs, cinnamon, and vanilla in a large bowl until well combined. Add the bread cubes and raisins and stir gently until the bread cubes are coated with the custard. Pour into an ungreased 1½-quart baking dish.

3. Bake until a knife inserted in the center of the pudding comes out clean, about 40 minutes.

4. Remove from the oven and let cool for 10 minutes. Serve warm.

### NUTRITIONAL INFORMATION

Serving Size: 1/10 recipe
Total Calories: 120
Calories from Fat: 20
Total Fat: 2 g
Saturated Fat: 1 g
Cholesterol: 45 mg

Sodium: 160 mg
Total Carbohydrates: 21 g
Dietary Fiber: 1 g
Sugars: 8 g
Protein: 5 g
**EXCHANGES PER SERVING**
1½ starches

# baked mango custard

Mangoes are a wonderful ingredient for desserts—their distinctive aroma and flavor blends so well with other components. Here, mango purée infuses baked custards. Don't bother unmolding them, and serve chilled, with a dollop of whipped topping and a couple of mango slices, if you so desire.

**2 ripe mangoes, peeled, pitted, and chopped (see page 83)**

**4 large eggs, at room temperature**

**½ cup SPLENDA® No Calorie Sweetener, Granulated**

**1 cup evaporated milk**

**1 teaspoon vanilla extract**

### NUTRITIONAL INFORMATION

Serving Size: 1 custard
Total Calories: 120
Calories from Fat: 45
Total Fat: 5 g
Saturated Fat: 2.5 g
Cholesterol: 115 mg

Sodium: 70 mg
Total Carbohydrates: 14 g
Dietary Fiber: 1 g
Sugars: 11 g
Protein: 6 g

**EXCHANGES PER SERVING**
1 starch, 1 fat

1. Position a rack in the center of the oven and preheat to 350°F.

2. Purée the chopped mangoes in a blender or a food processor. You should have about 1 cup purée.

3. Beat the eggs in a medium bowl with an electric mixer on medium speed until the eggs are frothy. Gradually beat in the SPLENDA® Granulated Sweetener. Gradually pour in the evaporated milk, mango purée, and vanilla. Pour the custard into eight 6-ounce custard cups or ramekins. Place the custard cups in a shallow roasting pan or baking dish.

4. Place the pan with the custard cups in the oven. Add enough hot water to come halfway up the sides of the cups. Bake until a knife inserted in the center of a custard comes out clean, 25 to 30 minutes.

5. Remove the custard cups from the water and transfer to wire racks. Let cool to room temperature. If desired, cover each cup with plastic wrap, pressing the plastic directly on the surface to prevent a skin from forming (see page 143), and refrigerate until chilled, at least 4 hours. Serve chilled or at room temperature.

# tiramisu trifle

Combining two favorite "spoon desserts" (a phrase often used by European cooks to denote soft, comforting sweets that are eaten most easily by the spoonful), this festive treat should be made a few hours before serving to allow the flavors to meld. Coffee, cocoa, cream cheese, and tender cake all come together in this marriage between Italian tiramisu and British trifle. For a large party, double the recipe and make in a trifle bowl.

**3½ teaspoons instant coffee**

**1½ cups boiling water**

**One 8-ounce package nonfat cream cheese, at room temperature**

**½ cup mascarpone cheese**

**1 cup SPLENDA® No Calorie Sweetener, Granulated**

**1 tablespoon SPLENDA® Brown Sugar Blend**

**½ teaspoon vanilla extract**

**1 purchased sugar-free angel food cake, cut into 1-inch cubes**

**2 teaspoons cocoa powder, divided**

1. Dissolve the coffee in the boiling water in a medium heatproof bowl. Place the bowl in a large bowl of iced water and let stand until the coffee is chilled.

2. Meanwhile, beat the cream cheese and mascarpone in a medium bowl with an electric mixer on low speed just until the cheese are blended. Add the SPLENDA® Granulated Sweetener, SPLENDA® Brown Sugar Blend, vanilla, and 2 tablespoons of the chilled coffee and mix until combined.

3. Pour half of the remaining chilled coffee into a 13-by-9-inch baking dish. Add half of the angel food cake cubes and mix quickly just until the cake absorbs the coffee. Place in a medium glass bowl. Spread half of the cheese mixture over the cake cubes. Sift 1 teaspoon of the cocoa powder over the cheese mixture. Repeat with the remaining coffee, cake, cheese mixture, and cocoa.

4. Cover tightly with plastic wrap and refrigerate until well chilled, at least 3 hours or overnight. Cut into squares and serve chilled.

**NUTRITIONAL INFORMATION**

| | |
|---|---|
| Serving Size: 1 square | Sodium: 350 mg |
| Total Calories: 190 | Total Carbohydrates: 25 g |
| Calories from Fat: 60 | Dietary Fiber: 0 g |
| Total Fat: 7 g | Sugars: 2 g |
| Saturated Fat: 4 g | Protein: 8 g |
| Cholesterol: 20 mg | **EXCHANGES PER SERVING** |
| | 1½ starch, 2 fats |

frozen desserts

# blueberry-sage granita

*Granita* is a frozen fruit dessert similar to sorbet, but its texture is refreshingly slushy. One major advantage is that it can be made right in your freezer without any special equipment. Make this version when blueberries are at their plumpest and sweetest.

**2 cups fresh blueberries**

**1¼ cups water**

**½ cup SPLENDA® No Calorie Sweetener, Granulated**

**1 tablespoon fresh orange juice**

**½ teaspoon ground sage**

**4 sprigs fresh sage for garnish**

### NUTRITIONAL INFORMATION

Serving Size: 1 serving
Total Calories: 60
Calories from Fat: 0
Total Fat: 0 g
Saturated Fat: 0 g
Cholesterol: 0 mg

Sodium: 0 mg
Total Carbohydrates: 14 g
Dietary Fiber: 2 g
Sugars: 8 g
Protein: 1 g

**EXCHANGES PER SERVING**
1 fruit

**1.** Chill an 8-inch square metal baking pan and a large metal serving spoon in the freezer.

**2.** Blend the blueberries, water, SPLENDA® Granulated Sweetener, orange juice, and sage in a blender until smooth. Pour into the chilled pan. Leave the spoon in the pan.

**3.** Freeze until the mixture is icy around the edges, about 1 hour, depending on the freezer's temperature. Using the metal spoon, mix the frozen edges into the center. Freeze, repeating the stirring procedure every 30 minutes and leaving the spoon in the pan, until the mixture has a slushy consistency, about 3 hours total freezing time. (The granita can be made up to 3 days ahead. Transfer the frozen granita to the refrigerator for 30 minutes before serving.)

**4.** Spoon the granita into chilled glasses and top with the sage sprigs. Serve immediately.

Use metal baking pans to make granitas and sorbets in the freezer, as these chill to a much colder temperature than glass dishes. The mixtures are stirred occasionally during freezing with a large metal serving spoon to give them their slushy texture. To keep the spoon as cold as possible, just leave it right in the pan and don't remove it between stirrings.

# orange arctic freeze

No matter what your level of cooking skill, all you need is patience and a few ingredients to create homemade orange sherbet. The mixture is first frozen solid, then beaten with an electric mixer, giving it a delectable, fluffy texture.

**1¼ cups SPLENDA® No Calorie Sweetener, Granulated**

**One 12-ounce container frozen orange juice, thawed**

**⅛ teaspoon salt**

**2 cups nonfat milk**

**One 12-ounce can evaporated milk**

**1 teaspoon vanilla extract**

NUTRITIONAL INFORMATION

Serving Size: ½ cup
Total Calories: 150
Calories from Fat: 25
Total Fat: 2.5 g
Saturated Fat: 2 g
Cholesterol: 15 mg

Sodium: 90 mg
Total Carbohydrates: 25 g
Dietary Fiber: 0 g
Sugars: 22 g
Protein: 5 g

EXCHANGES PER SERVING
1½ starches, 1 fat

1. Chill a 13-by-9-inch metal baking pan and a large stainless-steel mixing bowl in the freezer.

2. Mix the SPLENDA® Granulated Sweetener, orange juice, and salt in a medium bowl. Mix the nonfat milk, evaporated milk, and vanilla in another bowl. Gradually stir the orange juice mixture into the milk mixture. Pour into the chilled pan.

3. Cover with plastic wrap and freeze until solid, about 6 hours or overnight.

4. When ready to serve, cut the frozen mixture into chunks in the pan with a dinner knife. Transfer the chunks to the chilled bowl and beat with an electric mixer on high speed until fluffy. Transfer to an airtight container and freeze until firm again, about 1 hour. Serve frozen.

# key lime yogurt bars

The recipe for these tangy but sweet, frozen bars created by Carmela Barker of Cedarhurst, New York, was a winner in the SPLENDA® No Calorie Sweetener, Granulated Recipe Club Challenge. They are excellent for carefree summertime cooking, as they do not require any baking. While they are bars, they're easier to eat from a plate than out-of-hand.

Nonstick cooking spray for the pan

1 cup plus 4 tablespoons graham cracker crumbs (see page 127), divided

1¾ cups SPLENDA® No Calorie Sweetener, Granulated, divided

2 tablespoons margarine, melted

⅛ teaspoon ground cinnamon

⅓ cup Key lime juice, fresh or bottled (see Note)

2 cups plain low-fat yogurt

1 cup reduced-fat frozen whipped topping, thawed

### NUTRITIONAL INFORMATION

Serving Size: 1 bar
Total Calories: 150
Calories from Fat: 45
Total Fat: 5 g
Saturated Fat: 3 g
Cholesterol: 5 mg

Sodium: 150 mg
Total Carbohydrates: 22 g
Dietary Fiber: 0 g
Sugars: 5 g
Protein: 4 g

EXCHANGES PER SERVING
1½ starches, 1 fat

1. Spray the inside of an 8-inch square baking dish with the cooking spray.

2. In a small bowl, mix 1 cup plus 2 tablespoons of the graham cracker crumbs, ¼ cup of the SPLENDA® Granulated Sweetener, the melted margarine, and the cinnamon until the crumbs are evenly moistened. Press evenly into the bottom of the prepared pan.

3. Bring the remaining 1½ cups SPLENDA® and the lime juice to a boil in a medium saucepan over high heat, whisking to dissolve the SPLENDA®. Reduce to medium heat and boil until the mixture is reduced by half, about 5 minutes. Pour the lime mixture into a medium bowl and let cool completely.

4. Stir the yogurt into the lime mixture. Add the whipped topping and fold with a rubber spatula until combined. Spread evenly over the crust. Sprinkle with the remaining 2 tablespoons graham cracker crumbs. Cover with plastic wrap and freeze until firm, about 4 hours.

5. To serve, let stand at room temperature until very slightly softened, about 5 minutes. Using a sharp knife dipped into hot water, cut into bars. Serve frozen.

NOTE: Key limes are smaller and more aromatic than supermarket limes, and can be found during their summertime season in many produce markets. Carmela uses bottled Key lime juice, available at many supermarkets, but you can use fresh lime juice from either type of lime with great results.

# lemon sorbet

Lemon sorbet used to be served as a tart palate cleanser between courses of an elaborate meal. Now, it is most often offered at the end of a meal as a simple, palate-tingling dessert. The recipe gives instructions for using lemon shells for presentation, but the sorbet can also be spooned into small dishes.

**4 large lemons**

**4 cups boiling water**

**1 cup SPLENDA® No Calorie Sweetener, Granulated**

**Fresh mint sprigs for garnish (optional))**

### NUTRITIONAL INFORMATION

| | |
|---|---|
| Serving Size: ½ cup | Sodium: 0 mg |
| Total Calories: 25 | Total Carbohydrates: 6 g |
| Calories from Fat: 0 | Dietary Fiber: 0 g |
| Total Fat: 0 g | Sugars: 1 g |
| Saturated Fat: 0 g | Protein: 0 g |
| Cholesterol: 0 mg | EXCHANGES PER SERVING |
| | ½ fruit |

1. Chill a 9-inch square metal baking pan in the freezer.

2. Grate 1 tablespoon lemon zest from the lemons. Cut the lemons in half and squeeze to remove the juice, reserving the squeezed lemon halves. Strain the juice to remove any seeds. You should have ⅔ cup lemon juice. Scrape out the inside of each lemon with a dessert spoon to remove the pulp. Trim the bottoms from the lemon halves so they stand up.

3. Mix the boiling water and SPLENDA® Granulated Sweetener in a medium bowl. Let cool slightly. Stir in the lemon juice and zest. Pour into the chilled pan. Cover the pan with plastic wrap. Put the lemon halves in a zippered freezer-proof plastic bag.

4. Freeze the sorbet and lemon halves until solid, about 6 hours.

5. When ready to serve, put 8 dessert plates in the freezer to chill. Remove the pan from the freezer and let stand at room temperature until the sorbet begins to soften, about 10 minutes. Scrape the sorbet surface with a large metal spoon to give it a slushy consistency. Place a lemon half on each chilled plate. Heap lemon sorbet into each shell, garnish with mint sprigs, if using, and serve immediately.

# watermelon-raspberry ice pops

Remember back when summertime fun didn't get much better than trying to finish off a cool, sweet ice pop before it melted away? These tasty icicles are fashioned from two of the season's most popular fruits— watermelon and raspberries. You'll find ice pop molds and their wooden sticks at kitchenware shops.

**2 cups seeded and diced watermelon**

**1 cup fresh raspberries**

**⅓ cup SPLENDA® No Calorie Sweetener, Granulated**

**1 tablespoon fresh lemon juice**

**1 tablespoon light corn syrup**

**8 wooden sticks for the ice pop molds**

### NUTRITIONAL INFORMATION

| | |
|---|---|
| Serving Size: 1 pop | Sodium: 0 mg |
| Total Calories: 30 | Total Carbohydrates: 7 g |
| Calories from Fat: 0 | Dietary Fiber: 0 g |
| Total Fat: 0 g | Sugars: 5 g |
| Saturated Fat: 0 g | Protein: 0 g |
| Cholesterol: 0 mg | **EXCHANGES PER SERVING** |
| | ½ fruit |

1. Process the watermelon, raspberries, SPLENDA® Granulated Sweetener, lemon juice, and corn syrup in a food processor or blender until smooth. Rub the purée through a fine-mesh sieve into a small bowl to extract as much juice as possible. Discard the seeds and pulp in the sieve.

2. Divide the juice mixture among 8 ice pop molds and insert the sticks according to the manufacturer's directions. Freeze until the pops are solid, at least 6 hours or overnight.

3. To serve, dip the molds into a bowl of iced water for 10 seconds. Remove the pops from the molds and serve immediately.

You don't need an ice-cream maker to make many refreshing frozen desserts— granitas, slushes, sorbets, ice pops, and others can be produced just by means of your freezer. Their texture will be somewhat icy instead of smooth, but that only provides another layer of interest to the palate.

# raspberry ice

To end a sumptuous meal on a light, but festive note, serve scoops of this raspberry-orange ice in small dessert glasses. While fresh berries are preferred for many dishes, the frozen ones are excellent in ices and sauces.

**3 navel oranges**

**Three 12-ounce packages frozen unsweetened raspberries, thawed**

**1 cup SPLENDA® No Calorie Sweetener, Granulated**

**1 tablespoon fresh lemon juice**

**1 tablespoon grated orange zest**

**Thin strips of orange zest for garnish (optional)**

### NUTRITIONAL INFORMATION

Serving Size: ½ cup
Total Calories: 100
Calories from Fat: 0
Total Fat: 0 g
Saturated Fat: 0 g
Cholesterol: 0 mg

Sodium: 0 mg
Total Carbohydrates: 23 g
Dietary Fiber: 6 g
Sugars: 7 g
Protein: 1 g

EXCHANGES PER SERVING
1½ fruits

1. Chill an 8-inch square metal baking pan and a large stainless-steel mixing bowl in the freezer.

2. Grate 1 tablespoon zest from the oranges. Squeeze the juice from the oranges. You should have ¾ cup juice.

3. Process the raspberries, SPLENDA® Granulated Sweetener, orange juice, and lemon juice in a food processor fitted with the metal chopping blade or blender until smooth. Rub the purée through a fine-mesh sieve into a small bowl to extract as much juice as possible. Stir in the grated orange zest. Pour the juice mixture into the chilled pan. Discard the seeds and pulp in the sieve.

4. Cover the pan with plastic wrap and freeze until solid, about 6 hours or overnight.

5. When ready to serve, put 8 small dessert cups in the freezer to chill. Remove the pan from the freezer and let stand at room temperature until the raspberry ice begins to soften, about 10 minutes. Scrape the ice surface with a large metal spoon to give it a slushy consistency. Spoon the ice into each cup, garnish with a strip of orange zest, if desired, and serve immediately.

from the chefs

# kevin rathbun's apple-mint strudel

A popular European treat, strudel features fruit filling encased in crisp, paper-thin layers of filo dough. In this version from one of Atlanta's top chefs, Kevin Rathbun, fresh mint adds a refreshing note to apples. Be sure that the filo sheets are thoroughly defrosted overnight in the refrigerator.

**Nonstick cooking spray for the pan**

*Filling*

**4 Granny Smith apples, peeled, cored, chopped into ¾-inch cubes (4 cups)**

**¾ cup SPLENDA® Sugar Blend**

**2 tablespoons apple cider**

**½ cup all-purpose flour**

**2 tablespoons chopped fresh mint leaves**

**5 frozen filo pastry sheets, thawed overnight in the refrigerator**

**5 tablespoons unsalted butter, melted**

**2 tablespoons SPLENDA® Sugar Blend**

**Fresh berries and mint sprigs for garnish (optional)**

### NUTRITIONAL INFORMATION

Serving Size: 1 slice
Total Calories: 240
Calories from Fat: 70
Total Fat: 8 g
Saturated Fat: 4.5 g
Cholesterol: 20 mg

Sodium: 60 mg
Total Carbohydrates: 43 g
Dietary Fiber: 2 g
Sugars: 29 g
Protein: 2 g

**EXCHANGES PER SERVING**
2 starches, 1 fruit, 1 fat

1. Position a rack in the center of the oven and preheat to 375°F. Lightly spray a rimmed baking sheet with the cooking spray.

2. To make the filling, combine the apples, SPLENDA® Sugar Blend, and cider in a heavy saucepan over medium heat and cook, stirring occasionally, until the apples begin to turn translucent, about 8 minutes. Remove from the heat. Stir in the flour and mint.

3. Unfold the filo, stack the sheets, and cover the stack of sheets with a damp paper towel to keep them from drying out. Place a 16-inch-wide piece of waxed paper on the work surface, long side facing you. Remove 1 filo sheet of the stack and place on the waxed paper. Brush the filo with some of the melted butter and sprinkle with 1 tablespoon SPLENDA®. Repeat with the remaining 4 filo sheets.

4. Spoon the apple filling along the bottom edge of the stacked filo, leaving a 1-inch border at the bottom edge and the short sides. Fold in the short ends of the dough to cover 1 inch of the filling. Starting at the bottom edge, roll up the strudel, using the waxed paper as an aid. Do not roll it tightly or it may split during baking. Lift and transfer the strudel, seam side down, onto the prepared baking sheet. Discard the waxed paper. Cut ½-inch slits, about 1 inch apart, along the top of the strudel. Brush with the remaining butter and sprinkle with the remaining 1 tablepoon SPLENDA®.

5. Bake until the filo is golden brown, about 20 minutes. Let cool on the pan for 10 minutes, then cut into slices and serve warm.

# lorena garcia's tres leches cake with mango

In the center of Miami's Fashion District, the Food Café dishes up delicious food with a Latino accent, as one would expect considering the Venezuelan birthplace of the chef/owner, Lorena Garcia. *Tres leches* cake, made with three kinds of milk products combining to create a sweet soaking mixture for a vanilla cake, is popular throughout Latin America. Lorena adds an accent of color and flavor with fresh mangoes.

**Nonstick cooking spray for the pan**
*Cake*

**2 cups all-purpose flour**

**2 teaspoons baking soda**

**¾ cup SPLENDA® Sugar Blend**

**4 large eggs, separated, plus 2 large egg whites, at room temperature**

**1 teaspoon vanilla extract**

**½ cup nonfat milk**

**1 ripe mango, peeled, pitted, cut into ½-inch dice (1 cup, see page 83)**

**One 12-ounce can evaporated milk**

**One 14-ounce can condensed milk**

**1 pint fat-free half-and-half**

**2 tablespoons fresh orange juice**

**1 tablespoon SPLENDA® Sugar Blend**

**Reduced-fat frozen whipped topping, thawed, and unsweetened coconut flakes for garnish (optional)**

1. Position a rack in the center of the oven and preheat to 350°F. Spray the inside of a 9-inch springform pan with the cooking spray. Line the bottom of the pan with a round of waxed paper.

2. To make the cake, sift together the flour and baking soda into bowl. Stir in the SPLENDA® Sugar Blend. Beat the egg yolks and vanilla in a large bowl with an electric mixer on high speed until the yolks have tripled in volume and are pale yellow, about 3 minutes. On low speed, beat in three additions of the flour mixture, alternating with two additions of the milk, beating until smooth after each addition and scraping down the sides of the bowl often.

3. Using clean beaters in a clean bowl, beat the egg whites until soft peaks form. Stir one-fourth of the whites into the batter to lighten the mixture, then fold in the remaining whites. Spread evenly in the prepared pan.

4. Bake until the center of the cake springs back when pressed in the center, 35 to 45 minutes. Let cool in the pan on a wire rack for 5 minutes. Remove the sides of the pan. Invert the cake onto the rack, remove the bottom of the pan, and peel off the waxed paper. Turn right side up and let cool completely.

NUTRITIONAL INFORMATION

Serving Size: 1 slice
  without garnishes
Total Calories: 300
Calories from Fat: 30
Total Fat: 3.5 g
Saturated Fat: 0.5 g
Cholesterol: 85 mg

Sodium: 360 mg
Total Carbohydrates: 56 g
Dietary Fiber: 1 g
Sugars: 23 g
Protein: 10 g
EXCHANGES PER SERVING
3½ starches, 1 fat

5. Wash, dry, and reassemble the springform pan. Spread the mangoes in the pan. Place the cooled cake, right side up, in the pan and gently press to be sure the cake comes into contact with the mangoes. Pierce the top of the cake all over with a wooden skewer or meat fork. Place the pan in a larger roasting pan.

6. Whisk the evaporated milk, condensed milk, half-and-half, orange juice, and SPLENDA® Sugar Blend in a bowl. Slowly pour the milk mixture over the cake. Do not worry if the milk mixture leaks out of the springform pan, as it will be contained by the larger pan. Refrigerate until the cake has absorbed the milk mixture, at least 30 minutes or overnight.

7. To serve, remove the sides of the springform pan. Cut the cake into wedges and serve on dessert plates, being sure to include the mangoes. Top each serving with a dollop of whipped topping and a sprinkle of coconut, if desired.

# richard leach's eggnog cheesecake

The sweet creations of Richard Leach, long ensconced as the dessert wizard at Manhattan's Park Avenue Café, are famous for their unique combinations of the familiar with the unexpected. This lovely cheesecake, a perfect choice for holiday entertaining, is infused with the spirited flavors of eggnog.

### Crust

**Nonstick cooking spray for the pan**

**¾ cup plus 2 tablespoons graham cracker crumbs (see page 127)**

**5 tablespoons unsalted butter, melted**

**2 tablespoons SPLENDA® Sugar Blend**

### Filling

**12 ounces (about 1¼ cups) part-skim ricotta cheese**

**10 ounces nonfat cream cheese**

**One 8-ounce package cream cheese**

**⅓ cup plus 2 teaspoons SPLENDA® Sugar Blend**

**3 large eggs plus 3 large egg yolks**

**1½ teaspoons rum extract**

**½ teaspoon freshly grated nutmeg**

**½ vanilla bean, split lengthwise, seeds scraped from pod with the tip of a sharp knife**

1. Position a rack in the center of the oven and preheat to 325°F. Lightly spray the inside of an 8-inch round springform pan with the cooking spray. Wrap the bottom of the pan tightly in aluminum foil.

2. To make the crust, mix the graham cracker crumbs, melted butter, and SPLENDA® Sugar Blend in a medium bowl until the crumbs are evenly moistened. Press firmly and evenly into the pan.

3. Bake just until the edges of the crust are set, about 5 minutes. Transfer the pan to a wire rack. Reduce the oven temperature to 275°F.

4. To make the filling, combine the ricotta and cream cheeses in the bowl of a heavy-duty mixer fitted with the paddle blade. Beat on medium speed, scraping down the sides of the bowl often, just until the cheeses are combined and smooth. Reduce the speed to low and beat in the SPLENDA® Sugar Blend, whole eggs, egg yolks, rum extract, nutmeg, and vanilla seeds. Spread the filling in the prepared pan.

**5.** Place the springform pan in a larger roasting pan. Place the pan in the oven and add enough hot water to the roasting pan to come 1 inch up the sides of the springform pan. Bake for 45 minutes. Carefully rotate the pan from front to back and continue baking until the center of the cheesecake looks set, 30 to 45 minutes more.

**6.** Remove the springform pan from the roasting pan and transfer to a wire rack. Let cool to room temperature.

**7.** Cover the cheesecake with plastic wrap and refrigerate until chilled, at least 8 hours or overnight.

**8.** To serve, dip a sharp knife in hot water and run the knife around the inside of the pan to release the cheesecake. Dipping the knife into hot water between slices, cut the cake into wedges and serve chilled.

# adrián león's passion-apricot gelatins with red fruit sorbet

Adrián León is one the leading proponents of Nuevo Latino cuisine, where the foods of Latin America are used in exciting ways to create new dishes that have multicultural influences. This brilliantly colored mix of tropical fruit flavors is a perfect example of León's vibrant cooking. If you can't find prickly pears at your local Latino market, substitute an additional 1½ cups of mixed berries.

### Gelatins

**2 teaspoons unflavored gelatin**

**1 cup water, divided**

**½ cup canned or bottled passion fruit juice**

**½ cup canned apricot juice**

**1 cup SPLENDA® No Calorie Sweetener, Granulated**

**2 tablespoons fresh lemon juice**

1. To make the gelatins, sprinkle the gelatin over ¼ cup of the water in a medium bowl. Set aside for a few minutes for the water to absorb and soften the gelatin (see page 182).

2. Bring the remaining ¾ cup of water, passion fruit and apricot juices to a boil in a medium saucepan over high heat. Remove from the heat. Stir into the softened gelatin. Add the SPLENDA® Granulated Sweetener and lemon juice and stir until the gelatin is completely dissolved, at least 1 minute. Place the bowl in a larger bowl of iced water and let stand, stirring occasionally, just until the gelatin is the thickness of raw egg whites.

3. Pour equal amounts of the gelatin into 4 martini glasses or dessert cups. Cover each and refrigerate until the gelatin is chilled and set, at least 4 hours.

### Sorbet

1 cup water

1½ teaspoons fresh lemon juice

⅔ cup SPLENDA® No Calorie Sweetener, Granulated

2 ripe prickly pears

1 cup sliced strawberries

½ cup raspberries

NUTRITIONAL INFORMATION

Serving Size: 1 gelatin
  with sorbet
Total Calories: 130
Calories from Fat: 5
Total Fat: 0 g
Saturated Fat: 0 g
Cholesterol: 0 mg

Sodium: 10 mg
Total Carbohydrates: 36 g
Dietary Fiber: 3 g
Sugars: 6 g
Protein: 2 g

EXCHANGES PER SERVING
1 starch, 1½ fruits

4. Meanwhile, make the sorbet: Chill an 8-inch square metal baking pan and a large metal serving spoon in the freezer. Bring the water and lemon juice to a boil in a small saucepan over high heat. Remove from the heat. Add the SPLENDA® Granulated Sweetener and stir until it dissolves. Let cool completely. (Place the saucepan in the bowl of iced water, if you wish.)

5. Soak the prickly pears in a large bowl of cold water, which helps to loosen the remaining spines. Protecting your hand with a thick pot holder, pick up a pear. Use a paring knife to score the fruit into quadrants, cutting just through the skin to the flesh. Peel off the skin and coarsely chop the flesh.

6. In a food processor or blender, process the prickly pears, strawberries, raspberries, and cooled syrup until puréed. Pour into the chilled pan. Leave the spoon in the pan. Freeze until the mixture is icy around the edges, about 1 hour, depending on the freezer's temperature. Using the metal spoon, mix the frozen edges into the center. Freeze, repeating the stirring procedure every 30 minutes and leaving the spoon in the pan, until the mixture has a slushy consistency, about 3 hours total freezing time.

7. Top each gelatin with a scoop of red fruit sorbet. Serve immediately.

# stephan pyles's warm minted strawberry shortcakes

Stephan Pyles is widely recognized as one of the founding fathers of Southwestern cuisine, and he irrevocably altered the dining landscape of Dallas with his wonderful cooking. Here he makes strawberry shortcakes elegant by reducing the sugar and enlivens their flavor with fresh mint.

### Sweet Biscuits

**3 cups all-purpose flour**

**1½ tablespoons baking powder**

**1 teaspoon salt**

**1 cup SPLENDA® No Calorie Sweetener, Granulated**

**¾ cup trans-fat-free vegetable shortening**

**½ cup 2% reduced-fat milk**

**2 large eggs**

**2 tablespoons chopped fresh mint**

**Nonstick cooking spray for the baking sheet**

### Strawberries

**7 cups fresh strawberries, hulled and sliced**

**1 cup SPLENDA® No Calorie Sweetener, Granulated**

**2 tablespoons orange-flavored liqueur (optional)**

1. To make the biscuits, sift together the flour, baking powder, and salt into a medium bowl. Add the SPLENDA® Granulated Sweetener and mix well. Add the vegetable shortening and cut it into the flour with a pastry blender, two knives, or an electric mixer on low speed, until the mixture resembles coarse crumbs. Whisk the milk, eggs, and mint together in a bowl. Add to the dry ingredients and stir just until the dough comes together. Cover with plastic wrap and refrigerate until chilled, 30 minutes to 1 hour.

2. Meanwhile, prepare the strawberries: Place 5 cups of the strawberries in a medium bowl. Process the remaining 2 cups strawberries with the SPLENDA® Granulated Sweetner and liqueur, if using, in a food processor or blender until puréed. Pour over the sliced strawberries in the bowl and mix gently. Cover and refrigerate until ready to use.

## Sweetened Whipped Cream

½ cup heavy cream

¼ cup SPLENDA® No Calorie Sweetener, Granulated

1 teaspoon vanilla extract

**Fresh mint sprigs for garnish**

3. To make the whipped cream, combine the cream, SPLENDA® Granulated Sweetener, and vanilla in a chilled medium bowl and beat with an electric mixer on high speed until soft peaks form. Cover and refrigerate until ready to use.

4. Position a rack in the center of the oven and preheat to 325°F. Lightly spray a baking sheet with the cooking spray.

5. Turn out the dough onto a lightly floured work surface. Using floured hands, pat out the dough to ¾-inch thickness. Cut out shortcakes with a 3-inch round biscuit cutter, gathering up the scraps and gently patting them together as needed to make 8 shortcakes. Place the shortcakes on the prepared baking sheet.

6. Bake until the shortcakes are golden brown 20 to 25 minutes. Let cool on the pan for 2 to 3 minutes.

7. To serve, use a serrated knife to cut each hot shortcake in half crosswise. Place the bottom halves of the shortcakes on each of 8 serving plates and top with equal amounts of the strawberries and cream. Place the tops on the biscuits, garnish with the mint, and serve.

# rebecca rather's frozen peach yogurt

Any ice cream maker model, from the common ice-and-salt type to units with self-contained refrigerants, will work to whip up a batch of this creamy summertime extravagance, made lighter with low-fat dairy products and SPLENDA® Sugar Blend. This recipe comes from the extraordinary "Pastry Queen" Rebecca Rather, of Rather Sweet Bakery in the heart of Texas's Hill Country.

1½ cups low-fat evaporated milk

⅔ cup SPLENDA® Sugar Blend

3 large egg yolks

1 tablespoon vanilla extract

6 ripe peaches, peeled (see Note), pitted, sliced

Two 32-ounce containers plain low-fat yogurt

### NUTRITIONAL INFORMATION

Serving Size: ½ cup
Total Calories: 100
Calories from Fat: 20
Total Fat: 2 g
Saturated Fat: 1 g
Cholesterol: 30 mg

Sodium: 70 mg
Total Carbohydrates: 15 g
Dietary Fiber: 0 g
Sugars: 14 g
Protein: 6 g

**EXCHANGES PER SERVING**
1 low-fat milk

1. Whisk the evaporated milk, SPLENDA® Sugar Blend, and egg yolks in a medium saucepan until combined. Cook over medium heat, whisking constantly, until the mixture reaches 175°F on an instant-read thermometer. Strain through a fine-mesh sieve into a medium bowl. Stir in the vanilla. Place the bowl in a larger bowl of iced water and let stand, stirring often, until the custard stops steaming. Cover and refrigerate until chilled, about 2 hours.

2. In a food processor or blender, process the peaches until smooth. Transfer to another large bowl and stir in the yogurt. Cover and refrigerate until chilled, about 2 hours.

3. Combine the custard and peach mixture and mix well. In batches, transfer the peach custard to the container of an ice-cream maker and freeze according to the manufacturer's instructions (usually 30 to 40 minutes). Transfer the frozen yogurt to airtight containers and freeze until firm enough to scoop, about 1 hour. Serve frozen.

**NOTE:** To peel peaches, drop them in a saucepan of boiling water and cook until the skins loosen, about 1 minute or less. Drain and rinse under cold water. Use a small sharp knife to remove the skins.

# hans rockenwagner's macaroons with lemon crème

Hans Rockenwagner, one of California's most visible, popular, and accomplished chefs, contributed this European-style macaroon cookie. Instead of the American coconut version, these are made with a ground almond meringue, then sandwiched with a creamy lemon filling.

### Filling

5 large lemons

2 tablespoons cornstarch

½ cup SPLENDA® Sugar Blend

5 large egg yolks

¼ cup water

### Macaroons

1 cup SPLENDA® Sugar Blend, divided

1⅓ cups (6 ounces) almond flour (see Note)

1 tablespoon meringue powder (see Note)

5 large egg whites

½ teaspoon cream of tartar

1. To make the filling, grate 2 tablespoons lemon zest from 2 or 3 lemons. Juice the lemons and measure ¾ cup.

2. Pour the lemon juice into a medium, heavy-bottomed saucepan. Add the cornstarch and whisk until smooth. Add the SPLENDA® Sugar Blend, egg yolks, and water and whisk well. Cook over medium-low heat, stirring constantly with a wooden spatula, until the mixture is simmering and thick. Strain through a fine-mesh mesh sieve into a medium bowl. Stir in the lemon zest. Cover with plastic wrap, pressing the plastic directly on the surface (see page 143), and pierce with a few slits to allow the steam to escape. Let cool to room temperature. Refrigerate until chilled and firm enough to spread, at least 2 hours or overnight.

3. Line two baking sheets with parchment (baking) paper.

4. To make the macaroons, process the SPLENDA® Sugar Blend in a blender or food processor until powdery. Transfer half of the powdered SPLENDA® to a medium bowl, add the almond flour and dried meringue powder, and stir to combine.

5. In a bowl, beat the egg whites with an electric mixer on high speed until foamy. Add the cream of tartar and beat until soft peaks form. Gradually beat in the remaining powdered SPLENDA® until the whites form stiff, shiny peaks. Fold in the almond mixture.

6. Fit a pastry bag with a ½-inch plain tip. In batches, transfer the macaroon batter to the pastry bag and pipe out 150 quarter-sized mounds, 1 inch apart, onto the prepared baking sheets. Using a wet finger dipped in cold water, smooth down the pointed tail on each macaroon. Let stand uncovered for 20 minutes.

7. Position racks in the center and upper third of the oven and preheat to 325°F.

8. Bake until the macaroons are lightly browned on the bottoms (lift one gently with a spatula to check) and feel crisp, about 15 minutes. Let cool on the baking sheets on wire racks.

9. To assemble, sandwich the flat sides of 2 cookies together with about 1 teaspoon of the filling. Refrigerate in airtight containers until ready to serve.

NOTE: Almond flour, also called almond meal, can be found at specialty-food stores, some natural-foods stores, and online baker supply outlets. Meringue powders can be found at craft and cake decorating stores and in the bakery aisle of many supermarkets. They are used to make meringue and other foods where the egg whites would not be cooked to 160°F, the temperature at which many harmful bacteria are killed. A similar product, dried egg whites, may also be used.

# angela tustin's dried blueberry and lemon thyme scones

Philadelphia is gaining fame as one of America's great food towns, and it is the talents of chefs like Angela Tustin of Plate that are helping to spread the word. Angela is equally adept at both savory and dessert cooking, and these scones blend sweet and herbaceous elements to delicious effect. For a final fillip, spread your warm scone with the sweet lemon cream.

1½ cups cake flour (not self-rising)

½ cup all-purpose flour

2 teaspoons baking powder

½ teaspoon baking soda

¼ cup SPLENDA® Sugar Blend

½ cup (1 stick) unsalted butter, thinly sliced

¾ cup low-fat buttermilk

1 tablespoon freshly grated lemon zest

1 tablespoon fresh lemon thyme leaves (see Note)

½ cup dried blueberries or currants

1. Position a rack in the center of the oven and preheat to 425°F.

2. Sift together the cake flour, all-purpose flour, baking powder, and baking soda into a medium bowl. Stir in the SPLENDA® Sugar Blend. Add the butter and cut it in with a pastry blender, two knives, or an electric mixer on low speed until the mixture resembles coarse crumbs with some pea-sized pieces of butter. In a bowl, stir together the buttermilk, lemon zest, and thyme. Pour the buttermilk mixture into the dry ingredients. Add the blueberries and stir the dough just until the ingredients are barely combined.

3. Turn out the dough onto a lightly floured work surface. Gently knead the dough until it comes together, but do not overwork it. Using floured hands, pat the dough out to a ½-inch thickness. Cut out scones with a 2-inch round biscuit cutter, gathering up the scraps and gently patting them together as needed to make 15 scones. Place the scones 1 inch apart on an ungreased baking sheet.

4. Bake until the tops of the scones are golden brown, 10 to 12 minutes.

### Sweet Lemon Cream

**One 8-ounce container Neufchâtel cheese, at room temperature**

**3 tablespoons SPLENDA® Sugar Blend**

**3 tablespoons fresh lemon juice**

**2 teaspoons freshly grated lemon zest**

**¼ vanilla bean, split lengthwise, seeds scraped from the pod with the tip of a knife, or 1 teaspoon vanilla extract**

---

NUTRITIONAL INFORMATION

| | |
|---|---|
| Serving Size: 1 scone with lemon cream | Sodium: 450 mg |
| | Total Carbohydrates: 30 g |
| Total Calories: 240 | Dietary Fiber: 1 g |
| Calories from Fat: 110 | Sugars: 12 g |
| Total Fat: 12 g | Protein: 4 g |
| Saturated Fat: 8 g | EXCHANGES PER SERVING |
| Cholesterol: 35 mg | 2 starches, 2 fats |

**5.** Meanwhile, make the lemon cream: Beat the Neufchâtel, SPLENDA® Sugar Blend, lemon juice and zest, and vanilla seeds in a medium bowl with an electric mixer on medium speed until the mixture is fluffy. Transfer to a serving bowl.

**6.** Serve the scones warm, with the lemon cream.

**NOTE:** Lemon thyme has a distinct citrus fragrance. If you don't have it, substitute the leaves from 2 sprigs of regular thyme.

# bill yosses's candied apples

Bill Yosses may be one of New York City's premier pastry chefs and the creator of many unique and delicious desserts, but he hasn't forgotten the old-fashioned fun of biting into a sticky-chewy candied apple. The apples are best served within a few hours of making. Do not make the apples on a humid or rainy day, as the coating will quickly become too sticky after setting.

8 red apples

8 wooden dowels or ice pop sticks

Nonstick cooking spray for
   the waxed paper

2 cups SPLENDA® Sugar Blend

½ cup water

½ cup light corn syrup

2 tablespoons honey

1 tablespoon fresh lemon juice

6 to 8 drops red food coloring

### NUTRITIONAL INFORMATION

Serving Size:
  1 candied apple
Total Calories: 210
Calories from Fat: 0
Total Fat: 0 g
Saturated Fat: 0 g
Cholesterol: 0 mg

Sodium: 15 mg
Total Carbohydrates: 54 g
Dietary Fiber: 3 g
Sugars: 49 g
Protein: 0 g
**EXCHANGES PER SERVING**
2 starches, 1½ fruits

1. Wash and dry the apples. Insert a wooden dowel vertically into each apple at the apple's stem. Line a rimmed baking sheet with waxed paper and spray the waxed paper with nonstick cooking spray.

2. Combine the SPLENDA® Sugar Blend, water, corn syrup, honey, and lemon juice in a medium, heavy-bottomed saucepan. Attach a candy thermometer to the pan. Bring to a boil over high heat, stirring just until the SPLENDA® is dissolved. Boil, without stirring, until the syrup reaches 295°F. Remove the saucepan from the heat. Add the food coloring to reach the desired color, carefully swirling the pan by the handle to mix the syrup and coloring. Do not stir.

3. Put on rubber gloves to prevent burns from the very hot syrup. Working with one apple at a time, hold an apple by the wooden dowel and submerge the apple in the syrup to coat. If necessary, tilt the pan so the syrup pools to a good dipping depth. Hold the apple over the saucepan until the excess syrup stops dripping. Transfer the apple, stick end up, to the waxed paper. Let stand until the syrup hardens, at least 1 hour. The candied apples are best served within a few hours of making.

**NOTE:** The recipe includes extra syrup so the syrup is deep enough in the saucepan to easily dip the apples. To clean the saucepan after dipping the apples, immerse the cooled pot into a sink filled with hot water; the syrup will melt.

# gale gand's orange-vanilla panna cotta

Gale Gand, cookbook author, television chef, James Beard Pastry Chef of the Year in 2001, and creator of the exquisite desserts at Chicago's TRU restaurant, contributed this recipe for the classic, smooth-as-silk Italian pudding. *Panna cotta* means "cooked cream" in Italian, even though the "cream" is often actually milk, and it is not really cooked. But when a dessert is this good, who's to question?

**1 tablespoon unflavored gelatin**

**3 tablespoons water**

**4 cups whole milk**

**1 orange, zest removed with a vegetable peeler**

**½ vanilla bean (1 vanilla bean split lengthwise; half reserved for another use) or ½ teaspoon vanilla extract**

**½ cup SPLENDA® No Calorie Sweetener, Granulated**

**4 cups mixed fresh berries such as blueberries, raspberries, and sliced strawberries**

**1.** Sprinkle the gelatin over the water in a custard cup. Let stand without stirring until the gelatin absorbs the water, about 5 minutes.

**2.** Meanwhile, bring the milk, orange zest, and vanilla bean if using, to a simmer in a medium saucepan over medium heat. Remove the saucepan from the heat. Add the gelatin mixture and stir until the gelatin is completely dissolved, about 2 minutes. To test, rub a bit of the milk mixture between your thumb and forefinger. If it feels gritty, return the saucepan to very low heat and stir until the gelatin dissolves. Stir in the SPLENDA® Granulated Sweetener. Remove the vanilla bean from the hot milk and use the tip of a small sharp knife to scrape the vanilla seeds back into the milk (see Note). If using vanilla extract, stir it in now.

**3.** Strain the mixture into a large pitcher or a 1-quart measuring cup. Pour into eight 6-ounce ramekins or custard cups.

**4.** Cover each panna cotta with plastic wrap, pressing the plastic directly on the surface to prevent a skin from forming (see page 143). Refrigerate until chilled and set, at least 2 hours.

> CONTINUED

NUTRITIONAL INFORMATION

Serving Size: 1 custard
Total Calories: 110
Calories from Fat: 40
Total Fat: 4.5 g
Saturated Fat: 2.5 g
Cholesterol: 15 mg

Sodium: 65 mg
Total Carbohydrates: 13 g
Dietary Fiber: 2 g
Sugars: 10 g
Protein: 5 g

EXCHANGES PER SERVING
1 reduced-fat milk

5. To serve, fill a large bowl with hot water. Dip each ramekin into the hot water for 10 seconds; dry the outside of the ramekin with a kitchen towel. Using both thumbs, gently press around the edge of each panna cotta to loosen it from the ramekin. One at a time, invert a ramekin onto a dessert plate. Holding the ramekin and plate together, give them a sharp shake to unmold the custard from the ramekin, and remove the ramekin. Surround each panna cotta with about ½ cup of the berries. Serve chilled.

NOTE: Once the vanilla seeds have been removed from the bean, you can discard the bean. Better yet, rinse the bean and allow it to dry overnight. Bury the bean in a bag of SPLENDA® Granulated Sweetener and let stand for a week. The SPLENDA® will pick up the vanilla's aroma and a mild vanilla flavor that will allow you to slightly reduce the amount of vanilla extract in a recipe.

Gelatin is a somewhat temperamental ingredient, but it can be tamed. Sprinkle the gelatin over a small amount of cold water in a small bowl or custard cup and let it stand without stirring until the gelatin absorbs the water. This step, called "blooming," gives the gelatin an initial softening period. The softened gelatin is added to hot liquid and stirred well to thoroughly dissolve the gelatin. Do not be surprised if this takes a minute or two. Although hot liquid is used, the stirring is done off the heat, as overcooking will make the gelatin clump.

# acknowledgments

# photo credits

An entire team of people offering enthusiasm, support, and expertise compiled this book. Our sincere thanks go to everyone involved, with special gratitude to Judy Feagin, Jackie Mills, Johann Studier, MaryDawn Wright, and the celebrity chefs for their recipe development and culinary talents. Also thanks to Rick Rodgers for his passion for food and his ability to evoke enthusiasm via the written word.

*All photographs by Alison Miksch*
*unless otherwise indicated below*

Page 5: Photograph © Ann Menke 2004. Page 13: Photograph © Tony Anderson/Taxi collection/Getty Images. Page 33: Photograph © Sue Barr 2003, used with permission. Page 57: Photograph © Sue Barr 2000, used with permission. Page 77: Photograph © James Baigrie/Taxi Collection/Getty Images. Page 95: Photograph © Photolibrarycom/ Photonica collection/Getty Images. Page 111: Photograph © Sue Barr 2003, used with permission. Page 129: Photograph © Sue Barr 2003, used with permission. Page 139: Photograph © Sue Barr 2001, used with permission. Page 151: Photograph © Ariel Skelley/Blend Images collection/Getty Images. Page 161: Photograph © Jean Luc Morales/The Image Bank collection/Getty Images.